Simple
Sermons
for
Time and
Eternity

Simple Sermons for Time and Eternity

W. Herschel Ford

BAKER BOOK HOUSE
Grand Rapids, Michigan 49506

This book is lovingly dedicated
to
DR. J. CONALLY EVANS
faithful preacher of the Gospel of Christ,
devoted and dedicated servant of the Lord,
precious friend over the years,
and to his wonderful
WIFE AND CHILDREN

Introduction

God has given me the privilege of writing many books of "Simple Sermons." Here is another one, *Simple Sermons for Time and Eternity*, written with the hope and prayer that these messages will bless many people and bring many souls to Jesus.

One of these sermons bears the title, "From Sinking Sands He Lifted Me." A young preacher told me that he used this sermon in a revival service and twenty-one people made a profession of faith in Christ. I trust similar results will take place in other services.

Preachers and Christian workers are to feel free to use these messages in any way that will glorify God, win souls and bless lives.

W. Herschel Ford

Contents

1

Upward Steps in the Christian Life

1 Chronicles 29:1-13

God said that David was a man after His own heart. We know his life was not perfect, but we know that he loved God with all the fervor of his soul. He had one great ambition. He wanted to build a great temple for the Lord. He kept the dream alive in his heart down through the years. Now we see him as an old man. He doesn't have many days left on the earth. God speaks to him and says, "David, it is good that you had a dream in your heart to build a house for me. But you have been a warrior, a man of blood. You will not get to build that temple, but your son, Solomon, will build it in your stead."

Now we see David calling the people together in solemn conclave. He says to them, "All my life I have wanted to build a temple for the Lord. But that will not be my privilege. God has given that privilege to my son, Solomon. But before I die I want to make an offering for the building so that the work will go on after I am dead." Then he gave abundantly of his goods to the building fund. Then he said to the people, "Who then will consecrate his service this day unto the Lord?" In other words he said, "Who will join me in this offering?" The people responded nobly. They brought their gold and silver and iron and brass. Soon they had enough material to start the building. The people rejoiced. David rejoiced and praised the Lord.

Notice here the word "consecrate." What does it mean? It means "to set apart for God's use and God's service." This

9

is the highest step in the Christian life. Let us look at these steps today.

I. The First Step Is Salvation

The religious world is all mixed up on the matter of salvation. Instead of looking to the Bible they look to their own thoughts. Some people say that all men are the children of God. This simply means that they do not need salvation, they do not need the experience of conversion. They are saying that it was not necessary for Christ to come and die upon a cross, since all of us are saved anyway. Of course, this theory does away with all Bible truth. Some people say that we are saved by joining the church or going through a religious ceremony. They make the church a saviour, yet the Bible tells us that "there is none other name under heaven given among men, whereby we must be saved." Some people say that you are saved by good works. They think of salvation as a ladder. Every gift or good deed adds another rung. They hope to climb this ladder to heaven. Oh, so many people think of themselves in the matter of salvation instead of looking to Christ. Now what is involved in the matter of salvation?

1. *First, salvation indicates a lost condition.* This is the condition of all men without Christ. "He that believeth not the Son is condemned already." You look at yourself in the mirror and you say, "You are a pretty good fellow. There are many others worse than you." That may be true, but the fact still remains that without Christ you are eternally lost.

2. *Salvation indicates a consciousness of that lost condition.* This is what is meant by "conviction." The sinner must realize that he is lost. No one is ever saved until he knows that he is lost. In a revival a twelve-year-old boy came to the front of the church to accept Christ as his Saviour. His aunt came and sat by him. The big tears were running down his cheeks, so she said, "Sonny, why are you

crying?" And he replied, "Auntie, I am such a sinner, but I have given my heart to Christ and He has saved me." Then the Aunt said, "Sonny, you are not a sinner. You are not a bad boy — you are a good boy." "Auntie," said the boy, "you just don't know what you are talking about." And she didn't. She thought he could be saved by a good life, but the Holy Spirit showed the boy his sin and he knew he was lost.

3. *Then salvation involves a turning from sin.* No man is saved as long as he holds on to his sin. As conviction comes to him, he sees the wrong things in his life and he must say, "I am through with you. You are taking me to hell. But I am turning my back on you."

4. *Then salvation involves trusting Christ as Saviour.* Instead of turning to sin, you turn to a Saviour. Instead of holding on to sin, you take hold of Christ. It is a right-about-face experience. It is a turning from sin to the Saviour. A man loves a woman, he believes that she is a fine woman and will make him a good wife. But she does not become his wife until he stands before the preacher and receives her as his wife. You can believe everything wonderful about Jesus Christ, but you are never saved until you receive Him as your personal Saviour.

In the city of Jericho there lived a man by the name of Zacchaeus. He was a rich man. He got his money by collecting taxes for the Roman government and keeping a big cut for himself. One day Jesus came to the city. Zacchaeus heard about Him and wanted to see Him. He was too short to see Him above the heads of the crowd so he climbed up into a tree. When Jesus came along he stopped under that tree and invited Zacchaeus to come down. Zacchaeus came down and received Jesus gladly. He said, "I will sell half that I have and give to the poor. If I have wronged any man I will pay him fourfold." And Jesus said, "This day has salvation come to this house." Zacchaeus had felt his lost condition. He had turned from his sin. He had received Jesus as his Saviour.

The greatest experience in life is the experience of conversion. You come to realize that your sins have been forgiven. You realize that you are no longer a child of Satan, but a child of God. You realize that you are not on the road to hell, but you are on the road to the heavenly home. You realize that you are not alone, but that you have a divine Friend to walk with you down the pathway of life. Let us never forget the day of salvation. Let us often sing in our hearts, "O happy day that fixed my choice, on Thee my Saviour and my God."

II. The Second Upward Step Is the Step of Separation

When I speak of separation I do not mean Pharisaism. May the Lord deliver us from the Christian who thinks that everybody else falls short and that only he is perfect before God. There is no sweetness in a life like that. By separation I mean that there are some places to which a Christian cannot go, there are some things which a Christian cannot do. The world is looking at you and they need to see a difference in you.

You are a Christian and a member of the church, and one night you have company in for dinner. They are not church people, but they know that you are. You serve cocktails before dinner. What do they think of you and your Christianity? They know it is not genuine, because your life is no different from theirs. I have heard many women in our city say, "My husband is not a Christian. I am a church member and I have been living here for years, but my membership is still back home in another state." Now how can we win that husband? It is almost impossible to drag him over the barrier of his wife's indifference. He looks at her life and sees that it is no different from his. If he goes to hell, his blood will be on her hands. I tell you that the Christian must be different in every way.

Go to England and look at Queen Elizabeth. Do you
see her in the public saloons, drinking and carousing and
telling vulgar stories? No, she has a position to maintain
and she maintains it rigorously. In like manner the Christian has a position to maintain. He is a child of God and
he must live up to that position. A trucking company had
a certain sign on its gate. Every driver saw this sign as he
drove away. The sign bore the words, "Beyond this gate
you are the company." Beyond the doors of this church you
are the church. You are the representative of Jesus Christ.
Be careful how you live when you go out. It is not enough
just to come to church on Sunday and to give a little money.
Christianity ought to rule your everyday life and keep your
feet on the right path.

The poet said, "The world is too much with us." Yes,
and we are too much with the world, doing what the world
does, going where the world goes, indulging in the same
practices. But you will have no spiritual power and no
Christian influence until you build a fence between the
world and yourself. Then you are to get on the right side
of that fence. Don't judge others. Don't be critical of their
lives. Don't think you are better than they are, but quietly
take your stand by the side of Christ. Live a sweet, whole-
some, consecrated, happy, separated Christian life.

III. THE THIRD UPWARD STEP IS THE STEP OF CONSECRATION

Sometimes I dream of what I would like my church to
be. I would like for every member to live a good life, to
come to every service, to give God His tithe. I would like
for every member to serve where they are needed and to
witness for Christ every day. All of this can be summed up
by saying that I wish every member of my church was a
consecrated Christian.

1. *In consecration there should be a dedication of life.*
God may not call you to preach or to be a missionary, but
that doesn't mean that He hasn't called you to give your

life to Him. The business man, the professional man, the farmer, every man is called to give his life to Jesus. This does not mean that you will cease to be a business man, but that Christ will be first in your business. This does not mean that you cease to be a professional man, but that Christ will be first in your profession. This does not mean that you will cease to be a farmer, but it means that Christ will be first on your farm.

I often think of the kind of life I would try to live if I were not a preacher. I would probably be a business man. I know that I would pray and ask God to help me run my business. I would try to run the business honestly. I would try to set a Christian example for my employees and I would try to win them to Christ. I would be faithful to my church and give God a share of my income. I would go to church on Sunday and sit in a pew and pray for my pastor. I would look up into his face to receive the message God had given him for me. I would take a job in the church and give my best to it. I could run my business and still lead a life that was dedicated and consecrated to Christ.

2. *In consecration there should be dedicated talents.* Every good talent that is effective in the outside world could be put to good use in the church. We have a magician in our church who has real talent. He is one of the best. He not only uses his talent to help make a living, but he uses it for the glory of God also. Right here is the trouble with too many church members. They spread themselves out over too wide an area. The world calls and they answer and expend their energies there. They get a little recognition and their picture in the paper once in a while. But they miss many heavenly experiences. They use all their talents in causes that will die, instead of using them in the cause of Christ which will abide forever.

But someone says, "I don't have any talent to use for God." Well, listen to this story. Dwight L. Moody was preaching in a revival and a baby in the church began to cry. The mother quieted the baby, but soon it was crying again. The people around them became nervous and wondered why she wouldn't take the baby out. Moody stopped preaching and said, "Don't pay any attention to the baby. It does not bother me. But you are embarrassing the little mother. Maybe she could not have come to church if she couldn't have brought the baby. Then he turned to the mother and said, "Are you a Christian?" And she shook her head. Then Moody said, "There, she isn't a Christian, but she came to hear the Gospel." He didn't finish his sentence before a dozen women rushed over to take the baby and carry it out into another room. Moody didn't go on with his sermon, he just said, "This thing pleases God. A dozen people want to make it possible for one unsaved person to hear the Gospel and be saved." He gave the invitation and people crowded forward to accept Christ. The little mother was the first one to come. Oh, surely there is some little something you can do for Jesus if you dedicate your talents to Him and watch for an opportunity.

3. *In consecration there should be a dedication of time.* Here is a strange paradox in modern life. We have more time-saving devices than ever before, but less time for God. There was a time when the stores opened at six o'clock in the morning and closed at seven o'clock at night. On Saturday nights they were open until eleven o'clock at night. Many other businesses operated on the same schedule. But today we have a five-day week and most people work forty hours a week or less. Yet God doesn't get as much time from us as He formerly did.

You can't grow a great life unless you give some time to the culture of your soul. There should be time to pray, time for the Bible, time for the church, time for Christian service. No man ever became a great Christian by dropping into the church once a month and favoring God with an hour of his time.

4. *In consecration there should be a dedication of money.* Money is a vital part in every man's life. You are not stepping upward in the Christian life until you are doing the right thing with your money.

A certain preacher went with his wife to the ten-cent store. There he saw a little boy, ragged and dirty, looking longingly at the candy in the showcase. The preacher reached in his pocket, took out a quarter and gave it to the clerk, saying, "Give the boy a quarter's worth of candy and let him pick it out." The clerk smiled and said, "All right, son, what do you want?" Soon the boy had a bag full of candy and was cramming it into his mouth. The preacher said, "Is it good?" The boy said, "Uh huh," and kept on eating. The preacher held out his hand and said, "How about letting me have a piece?" The boy's expression changed. He clutched the bag tighter and cried out, "Mine, mine." Then he ran out of the store. That's the way some people treat God. He gives us everything and then when He asks us to give Him back a small part of it, we cry out, "Mine." We keep our part and God's part, too.

Dr. W. D. Nowlin was a pastor in Florida. He had a fine young man who served as Sunday school superintendent. This young man was a tither. Everyone liked him. He opened his own business and soon began to prosper. In a little while his tithe amounted to $100.00 per week. But he had become so busy that he had to give up his church work. Soon he opened up another business in another town and spent his weekends there. He quit coming to church. His tithe was still $100.00 per week. One day the preacher came to see him. He closed the door and sat down to talk to the young man. He said, "John, I am worried about you. You have been missing the church services. You seem to be losing interest in God's work and you are not giving Him all of your tithe." "Pastor," said the young man, "I thought one hundred dollars per week was too much to give to the church. And you know that my stores keep me mighty busy." Then the pastor said, "John, let us kneel in prayer." They knelt down and the pastor prayed, "Dear Lord, You have prospered John too much. You have given him too much business. He has had too much success. He says his tithe is too big to give to Thee. Dear Lord, for John's sake, burn down some of John's stores. Let some of them fail. Take away some of his business so that we can have the same John who used to love You and work for You so faithfully." John began to tremble, then he spoke out. "Pastor, let me take over from here." In his prayer he made a full confession. He asked God to forgive him. He promised that he would again tithe and that he would come back to the church. The next Sunday he was back on the job and again became the leading spirit in that church.

Oh, I wish that you could have a pastor's heart and feel as the pastor feels. I see many fine men and women who let the world get hold of them and I see them drift away from God. They fail to give God His tithe. But there is such joy and happiness when you are right with God in this respect. You ought to give God His tithe just for selfish reasons alone, because of the joy that would come back to you.

During the thirties a poor family lost all they had in the dust bowl of Oklahoma. They piled a few belongings in their old car and headed for the West Coast. The husband picked up enough work for them to get as far as Santa Fe, New Mexico. There a snow storm forced them to stop and they found lodging in a cheap tourist court. The wife was in the last stages of tuberculosis. She was taken to the charity hospital in the city. She asked the nurse to phone for a Baptist pastor and soon he came to the hospital. He found her dying, with her three poorly clad children by the bedside. She turned to one of the girls and said, "Sister, get Jesus' money for the pastor." The girl opened a battered suitcase, took out $3.57 and placed it in the pastor's hand. The woman said, "Pastor, this is the tithe of all the money my husband has been able to make since we left home. Put it in God's treasury. God will take care of my husband and the children when I have gone to glory. We love Jesus and we have tried to be faithful to Him."

A few days later the pastor stood in the pauper's cemetery with the husband and the weeping children. He committed the woman's body to the grave and her soul to the loving care of the Heavenly Father. And from out of the blue above the Sangre de Christo Mountains the pastor said that he seemed to hear the Heavenly Father saying, "Well done, thou good and faithful servant. Enter thou into the joys of thy Lord."

Oh, I tell you, I had rather be that poor woman lying in a pauper's grave than to be some people who live in comfortable homes, who have all the conveniences of life and yet who do not know the joy of doing God's will in the matter of money.

IV. The Last Step Is the Step of Glorification

God gives salvation, then comes separation from the world, then comes dedication and at the end of the way comes glorification. The old song says, "He will give me grace and glory." He gives the grace here and the glory there. Another song says, "Oh, that will be glory for me, when by His grace I shall look on His face, that will be glory for me'.'

Yes, Christ promises to share His heavenly glory with all those who trust Him. On the Isle of Patmos God pulled back the curtain of eternity and showed John all the glories of heaven. The sight was so glorious that John didn't want to stay down here. He cried out for Jesus to come and take him home. If you and I knew all that is waiting for us up in heaven we, too, would want to leave this old sinful earth and go up to be at home with Jesus. A poor old lady lay dying in the county poorhouse. The doctor heard her whisper, "Praise the Lord, praise the Lord." "Why, auntie," said the doctor, "how can you praise the Lord when you are dying here in the poorhouse?" "Oh, doctor," she said, "it is wonderful to go from the poorhouse to a mansion in the sky."

Dr. Porter Routh is one of our great Southern Baptist leaders. When he was a boy he lived in El Paso for a time. While here he was saved and baptized into the fellowship of First Baptist Church. At that time his mother was very ill. One Sunday the pastor asked Dr. Routh's father to preach for him. When Porter arrived home after church he went into his mother's room and she said, "Porter, what did your father preach about this morning?" He said, "He preached about abiding things, faith, hope, salvation, Christ." "Yes, son, these are the only things that abide." Porter then went on into the dining room to eat his Sunday dinner. When he went back to his mother's room she had gone out to be with God.

My friends, the only thing that counts is our faith and love and hope in Christ. I beg you to get on the road of a consecrated Christian life. Climb the steps with Jesus. Then at the end of the way you will find all the glory and joy of heaven for which you have been waiting.

2

The Greatest School in the World

Matthew 11:29

Every person in the world is a learner. From the cradle to the grave we are continually learning the great lessons of life. We have some marvelous teachers — experience, sorrow, example, communion with God and fellowship with the great people of the world. But today I want to tell you of the greatest school in all the world. It is the school where Christ is the Teacher. He is the Master Teacher of all the ages. It was said of Him that "He spoke as never man had spoken before." It was said of Him that "He spoke as One having authority." After all these years we still need to sit at His feet and learn the great lessons of life.

Jesus knows more about the stars than the greatest astronomer. He knows more about the flowers than the greatest botanist. He knows more about the human body than the greatest physician. He knows more about the world than the greatest traveler. He knows more about the soul than the greatest theologian.

Education has made great strides in the last one hundred years. In those days a school consisted of a log cabin in the country. A school had one teacher and she taught all subjects to all ages. Yet some of the greatest men and women America has ever produced have come out of those schools. Today we have our fine buildings. Today we have our large endowments. Today we have trained teachers who specialize in certain subjects. Any boy or girl today can go to the highest university. Yet there is no school in the world to compare with the school of Christ.

I can see Him now as He stands before His class in those days so long ago. He has been talking about the great themes of time and eternity. I hear Him say, "Come unto Me all ye that labour and are heavily laden." Then I hear Him say, "Take my yoke upon you and learn of me." And over the years the men of this world have learned their greatest lessons at the feet of Jesus. Let us think today of some of these lessons.

I. In the School of Christ We Learn to Know the Teacher

The most important thing about a school is its teacher. Buildings are not the most important things. I can remember years ago visiting some of the small mountain schools that we had in the Southland. The buildings were old and inadequate, but inside of those buildings good Christian teachers were teaching the great truths of God and preparing boys and girls to go out into the world and make it a better place in which to live. Books are not the most important things about a school. Some years ago the president of one of our fine Christian schools in the South was attending a banquet of educators in New York City. The president of a northern school said to him, "How can we have a real Christian school? History is the same in every school, science is the same, mathematics is the same. How can you make your school Christian?" And the good man answered, "First of all you must have Christian teachers." Yes, it is the teacher who makes the school. They were having a revival meeting adjacent to the campus of that same southern school. The school was dismissed each morning at chapel time so that the students could attend the morning service. Just before the bell rang the chemistry teacher erased everything that was on the blackboard. That morning he had been talking about the chemistry of the blood. He then wrote upon the blackboard these words, "The blood of Jesus Christ His Son cleanses us from all sin." That's the kind of teacher it takes to make a Christian school.

Neither is it the size of the school which is the most important thing. Some of the finest leaders in the world have come out of the smallest schools. The teacher is the important thing about any school. Give us the right kind of teachers and then it will not matter about the buildings, the books or the size of the school.

There are two kinds of knowledge, hearsay and experimental. An old man and his son stood before the statue of a great general. The son said, "Father, I know about that man. I studied about him in history." And the father said, "But I knew him personally. I followed him in many battles." One knew the general historically, the other knew him personally. This is one blessed thing about the school of Christ. We come to know the Great Teacher personally.

An actor in a certain group was called upon to recite the twenty-third Psalm. He gave a flawless performance. An old preacher was present and the actor insisted that he recite the twenty-third Psalm. The preacher did this and at the close of the recital there were tears in the eyes of the actor. He said to the preacher, "I know the Psalm, but you know the Shepherd." In the school of Christ we come to know, not only the great lessons of life, but we come to know the Teacher, the Great Shepherd.

In our schools different teachers teach different subjects. There is only one subject in the school of Christ and that is the subject of human conduct. Jesus teaches us to have the right attitudes toward God and our fellow man. He was not indifferent to others things, but He knew that if He could get men into right relationship with God and man, all of life would take on new meaning. Jesus was the Master Teacher and He teaches the best lessons. But that is not all. In His school we learn to know Him in the sweetness and beauty of His wonderful character.

II. In the School of Christ We Learn to Pray

We learned to say prayers at our mother's knee, but in the school of Christ we really learn to pray. When I was a boy I prayed for some ridiculous things, but when I came to know Christ I learned to pray in a better way. The disciples said, "Lord, teach us to pray." He does just that in His classroom. I would rather know how to pray than to know how to preach. I would rather know how to pray than to know how to sing. I would rather know how to pray than to know how to teach. I can't do any of these things unless I pray. I can do nothing well until I have prayed about it.

The most serious indictment that can be brought against any of us is that we do not pray enough. We know about the prayer promises in the Bible, we know the power of prayer, we know the experience that we have had in prayer in days gone by. But we don't pray as we should. We often slip downward and away from Christ and sometimes into sin because we do not pray. I have seen hundreds of active and faithful church members give up all of their Christian activities and go back into the world. I know one thing about them. I know that they don't really pray or their lives would be changed.

A certain Christian was out of our country for twenty-five years. When he returned he visited in many places. Someone said to him, "What is the greatest change you have seen in America?" They thought he would talk about the tall skyscrapers, the marvels of television, the jet planes, the changes in our economic system. But he didn't mention these things. He said, "The greatest change I have seen is that people do not pray as they did in other days. No longer do they have a family altar in the home."

James Gilmour was a pioneer missionary to Mongolia. He was a mighty man of prayer. He never used a blotter when he wrote a letter. He prayed while waiting for the ink to dry. Time spent in prayer is never wasted. We learn to pray in the school of Christ.

III. In the School of Christ We Learn to Trust Him

Job went to this school and the teacher gave him some difficult assignments. He lost his property, he lost his family, he lost his health. He was plowed under with grief and sorrow. His wife came to him and said, "You have been serving God all of these years and you have gotten nothing out of it. Why don't you curse God and die?" But Job rose up in great faith and said, "Though He slay me, yet will I trust Him." He learned the great lesson of trust and in the days to come God really blessed him.

Faith has done many things in the world, but unbelief has nothing good to its credit. Faith has built churches and schools and hospitals and children's homes. Unbelief has done nothing good.

The Jackson family, some of our missionaries in Brazil, were on the way home on the steamship *Vestriss*. The ship sank and Mr. and Mrs. Jackson and their son were drowned. The Jacksons had a daughter in the seminary at Forth Worth. The ladies of the Gaston Avenue Baptist Church in Dallas had taken this daughter as their special project. They were helping her to get her education so that she might become a missionary. When the tragedy struck, some of the good women went over to Fort Worth and brought this daughter to Dallas. They gave her all of their love and sympathy and said to her, "What can we do for you now?" She said, "I am all right. I don't understand all of this, but my faith is not weakened. There is no question in my heart. I know that all things work together for good to them that love God." Oh, for a mighty faith like that!

During the depression days of the 30's I knew two types of men. One man said, "I have lost everything, now life is not worthy living any more." Then this man ended his life The other man said, "I have lost everything but God. I still have faith in Him. I will trust Him to work things out all right for me."

One day a terrific storm was raging and two little children in a certain house were sore afraid and were crying out in their fear. Then a little five-year-old said to them, "Stop bawling, don't you suppose God knows His business?" He does know His business. He will do the right thing.

We can trust Him. We learn to trust Him in the school of Christ.

IV. IN THE SCHOOL OF CHRIST WE LEARN THE SPIRIT OF CHRIST

What is the Christ spirit? It is the spirit of love and forgiveness toward others. I am afraid that few Christians have that spirit today. Yet we have a chance to use it every day. But not many people are big enough to put others first and to forget all the little slights of life. When a thing like this comes up they let the spirit of the devil rule them instead of the spirit of Christ. But after all the thing that counts in a man is his spirit. If a man has the right spirit you don't have to worry about his actions. If his spirit is right he will do that which is right. And you can't live close to Christ and have a spiteful, hateful spirit. If you have the wrong attitude and a bitter feeling toward others in your heart, you need to go back and learn from Christ, who, when He was reviled, reviled not back again.

Some years ago in the Southern Baptist Convention a Chinese preacher stood up to speak. He began his speech by saying, "Brothers and sisters in Jesus Christ." And I thought that if a man who had come out of heathenism could exhibit a beautiful spirit like that, how much more should we who have known Christ all of our lives and who have been so greatly blessed of Him, exhibit the Christ spirit.

You and I are to look upon all the people in the world in love and in the spirit of Christ. Yes, we learn of His spirit in His school.

V. IN THE SCHOOL OF CHRIST WE LEARN OF HIS SUFFERING, HIS DEATH AND HIS POWER OVER THE GRAVE

At the close of the war Dr. Daniel Poling went down to the docks and watched the soldiers as they raced down the gangplanks of the ships and into the arms of their loved ones. One day he saw a mother looking for her boy. Suddenly she said, "There he is," and in a moment they were in each other's arms. Then that boy said, "Wait a minute." He went back and took another soldier by the hand and led him to his mother. "Here he is, mother," said the boy. "He is my best friend. We went over the top together. An enemy soldier pointed his gun at me, but this friend leaped in front of me and received the full charge of the gun. Now he is blind. He did it all for me." And that mother, with tears in her eyes, touched those blinded eyes and said, "Thank you, thank you for what you did for my boy and for me." Oh, Jesus at Calvary took suffering and death for you and me. Surely we want to fall at His feet and thank Him for all that He did for us.

There was One who was willing to die in my stead
  That a soul so unworthy might live,
And the path to the cross He was willing to tread
  All the sins of my life to forgive.

He is tender and loving and patient with me,
  While He cleanses my heart of its dross,
But there's no condemnation, I know I am free,
  For my sins are all nailed to the cross.

I will cling to my Saviour and never depart,
  I will joyfully journey each day,
With a song on my lips and a song in my heart,
  That my sins have been taken away.

They are nailed to the cross, they are nailed to the cross,
  Oh, how much He was willing to bear,
With what anguish and loss Jesus went to the cross,
  But He carried my sins with Him there.

But when we go past the cross we come to an empty tomb. We thank God that that tomb is empty. We learn that He is a risen Saviour. We are not depending upon a dead God. We learn all of this in the school of Christ.

VI. In the School of Christ We Learn of the Glorious Home Prepared for the Redeemed

He said, "I go to prepare a place for you. And if I go and prepare a place for you, I will come again, and receive you unto myself; that where I am, there ye may be also." A preacher visited a woman on her eighty-eighth birthday. He said to her, "I wish you many more years of life." "Don't wish that," she said. "I want to go on and be with Jesus. Look at this old house. The roof is leaking and the porch is falling in. I want to say good-by to this little shack and go on up to the house not made with hands." Yes, life in the school of Christ grows sweeter and finer and better every day. But one day we will graduate into heaven. Then "the toils of the road will seem nothing, when we get to the end of the way."

Wendell Phillips, the great reformer, one night made a speech in a town some miles from his Boston home. Afterward a friend said to him, "The last train has gone. If you go now you must go in a carriage. It will be a hard journey. The weather is cold and raw. Spend the night with us and take the train in the morning." And Mr. Phillips answered, "Thank you, but I must go home tonight. For at the end of those miles Ann Phillips is waiting for me." Life is often hard and full of trouble, but it is sweet to know that Jesus and heaven wait for us at the end of the way.

Some years ago I was traveling a rough mountain road. I stopped and asked a farmer for directions. After he had given me these directions I said, "This is a pretty rough road, isn't it?" And he said, "Yes, but it is better farther on." And I found it so. Is life hard for you? Is it filled with many cares? Well, here is comfort for you. It is better farther on.

VII. If We Have Learned These Lessons in His School, Then Two Things Will Result

First, we will walk with Him in perfect trust. We will realize that we are never alone. We will come to know that He will never permit anything to overcome us.

Second, we will become more consecrated. In His school we learn what He did for us, what He is doing for us and what He is going to do for us. Then if there is any gratitude in us at all, we will want to live better lives for Him. The highest gift to Him and to the world is the gift of self. The distinguishing mark of Christ's followers is that they give of themselves.

In World War I, a soldier said to President Wilson, "We are ready to do your bidding, if it takes the last drop of our blood and the last man of us." That is full consecration. When Texas came to her finest and most dangerous hour Colonel Travis said, "We will never surrender nor retreat." That is full consecration. Someone spoke to David Livingstone about the sacrifice he had made in Africa and he replied, "Is it a sacrifice to pay a little part of the great debt that I owe to the Lord Jesus Christ?" That is full consecration.

Over in India a missionary saw a woman going toward a heathen temple one morning. She had two children with her. One was crippled and blind and the other was a strong, beautiful, well-formed child. "Where are you going?" he asked. And she said, "I am going to the temple to make a sacrifice to my gods." That afternoon he saw her coming back. The crippled child was with her, but the strong and beautiful child was nowhere to be seen. The missionary asked her the question, "Where is your other child?" And she said, "I sacrificed him to my gods today." Then the missionary said, "If you were going to make a human sacrifice, why did you not sacrifice the blind and crippled child?" And she answered, "Oh no, we give our best to our gods. This may be too much for you Christians, but it is not too much for us."

What a rebuke! I wonder how much of yourself you are giving to Christ. The best we can give is not too much to give Him who gave His all for us.

3

What Is Happiness?

John 10:10

There are various types of happiness. There is the happiness of wealth, the happiness of health, the happiness of family, the happiness of friends, the happiness of achievement. But spiritual happiness is the only type of permanent happiness. Lasting happiness must spring from the things of the spirit.

I. HAPPINESS IS KNOWING THAT GOD IS YOUR FATHER

We have a false idea abroad in the land today. Many people who have not studied their Bibles glibly talk about the "Fatherhood of God," inferring that God is the spiritual Father of all people. Yet Jesus said to a certain group, "Ye are of your father, the devil." We are born in sin and God is not our Father until we are born again. John 1:12 says, "As many as received Him, to them gave He power to become the sons of God." This verse implies that those who have not received Christ are not the children of God. All men are the children of God in the creative sense but not in a redemptive sense.

My earthly father was not prominent or rich or well-known. But he had a reputation for honesty and integrity and hard work. I am proud to be the son of such a man. But when I think of God, of His greatness and goodness and grace, I can say with the Psalmist, "There is no God like unto our God." We can be proud to be the sons of God through our faith in the Lord Jesus Christ.

The pastor of one of our great churches recently stated

in his bulletin that they had a few well-to-do people in the
membership, but that the majority of them were plain, everyday, hard-working people. Someone said to a woman in
that church, "Your church is full of rich people." And this
woman, who is very poor, replied, "Yes, and I am the richest
one of them all." She felt that she was rich because God was
her Father.

> My Father is rich in houses and lands,
> He holdeth the wealth of the world in His hands,
> Of rubies and diamonds, of silver and gold,
> His coffers are full, He has riches untold.
>
> My Father's own Son, the Saviour of men,
> Once wandered on earth as the poorest of them
> But now He is pleading our pardon on high.
> That we may be His when He comes by and by.
>
> I once was an outcast stranger on earth,
> A sinner by choice, and an alien by birth;
> But I've been adopted, my name's written down,
> An heir to a mansion, a robe, and a crown.
>
> A tent or a cottage, why should I care?
> They're building a mansion for me over there;
> Tho' exiled from home, yet, still I may sing,
> All glory to God, I'm a child of the King.
>
> I'm a child of the King, a child of the King;
> With Jesus my Saviour, I'm a child of the King.

Certainly it is happiness to know that you are a child
of God. It is happiness to know that He loves you with all
of His heart. It is happiness to know that you can always
call on Him, to know that He is always ready to pour out
His blessings upon you. It is happiness to know that He
cares for us more tenderly than any earthly father cares for
his child.

II. Happiness Is Knowing That Christ Is Your Saviour

The Trinity is a mystery. It is hard for us to understand the existence of three persons in one. But in our daily
thinking, without theological arguments, we think of God
as our Father and of Christ as a separate Being, our Saviour.

If we are wrong in thinking this way, surely God will not hold it against us. Now it is happiness to know that one day you repented of your sins and put your faith in that Saviour. Now He is not just the Saviour of the world, but He is a personal Saviour. The world is full of people who can't say, "He is mine." They are missing life's greatest joy. They are the poorest people in the world.

A missionary was speaking to a group of fishermen in Labrador. He tried to tell them what Christ's death on the cross meant. At the end of his message he asked the question, "Will you tell me in your own words what Christ did when He died on the cross?" One old man, with tears coursing down his cheeks, said, "I just now saw what He did. He swapped places with me. He took my place on the cross and left me here, a sinner saved by grace." Yes, Jesus swapped with us. One day I accepted His call. I came to Him with my sin. He said, "Give me your sin and I will give you My salvation." And when I did that I was saved. My heart overflowed with joy, my soul was filled with hope.

We can't understand all of this, but thank God it happens. Jesus one day gave a blind man his sight. When someone asked him how it happened he could not explain it. He simply said, "I don't know all about it, but I do know this one thing. Once I was blind, but now I see."

> Amazing grace! how sweet the sound,
> That saved a wretch like me!
> I once was lost, but now am found,
> Was blind, but now I see.

Yes, it is happiness to know that God is our Father and Christ is our Saviour. Nothing in the world can break that tie. Paul said, "I am persuaded, that neither death, nor life, nor angels, nor principalities, nor powers, nor things present, nor things to come, nor height, nor depth, nor any other creature, shall be able to separate us from the love of God, which is in Christ Jesus our Lord."

III. Happiness Is Knowing That the Holy Spirit Dwells Within

Here is a lovely house being occupied by some unlovely people. Then one day they are forced to move out and a wonderful family moves in. The heart of a Christian was once filled with sin and unlovely things. Then one day Jesus moved in. He forced the unlovely things out and the Holy Spirit came in to dwell forever. And He is there now, to comfort, to guide and to strengthen.

A few months ago two sisters died together in Belmont, California. One of them was eighty-four years of age, the other was seventy-five. The younger one had the mind of a child. She always called her sister "mother." She begged her never to leave her. They were always together. They went from one rest home to another. The time came when the older sister knew that younger one would have to go to a sanitarium. They would then be separated for the first time in their lives. The younger sister sobbed out, "You won't leave me, will you, mother?" And the older sister replied, "Of course not. I told you that we would never be separated." They went for a walk in the garden and the next morning both of their bodies were found there, a bullet through their heads. The older sister had killed the younger one and herself so that they would never be separated.

Now human beings may resort to such measures to stay together, but the Christian has no such problem. He knows that the Holy Spirit will never leave him. He will abide with him forever. The Holy Spirit is truly God living in the heart. He comes in at conversion and never leaves.

IV. Happiness Is Knowing That Your Sins Have Been Forgiven

Of course the old sin of the Adamic nature is forgiven when you come to Christ. But I speak now of the sins which we commit as Christians. When we sin we are not happy. If we are real Christians, we become miserable over our sin. When we see our sins, we cry out to God and He quickly forgives. John was talking about this when he said, "If we confess our sins, He is faithful and just to forgive us our sins, and to cleanse us from all unrighteousness." Of course, this means more than making an oral confession. It means forsaking that sin and turning away from it.

Simon Peter was a Christian, but one night he committed a grievous sin. He swore and declared that he had never known Jesus. Was he happy about it? No, he went out and wept bitterly. If you are a Christian and if you sin, you will not be happy about it either. What did Simon Peter do about it? He didn't stay in sin. He came back to Jesus and declared his love for Him. His sin was forgiven and he became a happy and effective Christian.

Take the case of David. If ever a man plumbed to the depths of both sainthood and sin, he did. He was called a man after God's own heart, but he committed an awful sin. One day he saw a beautiful woman at her bath. He coveted her and looked upon her lustfully. He took her to himself and broke the seventh commandment. Then he sent her husband into the front-line trenches where he knew that he would be killed. When he heard of the husband's death, he took the woman for himself. Look at the commandments that he violated. He put the god of lust before the God of heaven. He coveted his neighbor's wife. He committed adultery. He committed murder. Now was he happy afterwards? No, he said that his very bones ached over his sin. So what did he do about it? He came to God in humility. He poured out his heart, telling God how he had sinned and how sorry he was because of it. He didn't blame someone else. He simply cried out to God to forgive him and to give back to him the joy of his salvation. You see, he had not lost his salvation, but only the joy of it.

And God forgave David and washed him clean. Listen to him now as he says, "Happy is the man whose transgression is forgiven, whose sin is covered." He was simply saying, "I am happy now because God has forgiven my sin and restored to me the joy of my salvation."

Do you have any sins that you are carrying around with you? Is there something between you and God? It may be a sin of the flesh or a sin of commission. It may be a sin of omission, which means that you are not doing what you should. It may be a sin of disposition, you may have the wrong feeling toward someone else. You can't be happy until you get rid of that sin. So come to Christ and you will find Him waiting to forgive you. Yes, happiness is knowing that your sins have been forgiven.

V. HAPPINESS IS KNOWING THAT YOU HAVE A GOOD CHURCH HOME

The church is the greatest institution in the world. It is the only one founded by the Lord Jesus Himself. It is a joy and a privilege to be a member of a real New Testament church. The church should have first claim upon your time and life. It should be sustained in your prayers and supported by your gifts.

There are many people in the world who are far removed from any church. They would be happy to have the privilege that is yours, the privilege of membership and service and fellowship in a good church. Oh, let us be faithful to the church, the institution that is seeking to carry out God's will in the world.

VI. HAPPINESS IS KNOWING THAT YOU HAVE THE PRIVILEGE OF PRAYER

Suppose that some power could cut you off from God so that you couldn't come to Him in prayer. Then when you sinned there would be no way to ask for forgiveness. When you were sick there would be no way to ask for help. When you were in sorrow there would be no way to ask for comfort. All of this would be tragic, wouldn't it?

I believe that prayer makes us better people. I believe

that if we prayed as individuals, we would grow in grace. I believe that if we prayed as a church, we would see many mighty things coming to pass. Oh, the great trouble with Christians is that they pray so little. If every Christian in the world went aside for a season of private prayer every day, I believe that we would have a different world. Yes, happiness is knowing that you have the privilege of prayer.

VII. Happiness Is Knowing That You Have the Bible as Your Guide

If you were going to drive tomorrow over the strange roads to a distant city where you had never been, you would call for a road map to guide you. Well, the Bible is the guidebook from doom to glory, from earth to heaven, through all the dark valleys. Listen to what Billy Sunday said about the Bible.

Twenty-nine years ago with the Holy Spirit as my Guide, I entered at the portico of Genesis, walked down the corridor of the Old Testament art galleries, where pictures of Noah, Abraham, Moses, Joseph, Isaac, and Jacob, and Daniel hung on the wall. I passed into the music room of the Psalms where the Spirit sweeps the keyboard of nature until it seems that every reed and pipe in God's great organ responds to the harp of David, the sweet-singer of Israel.

I entered the chamber of Ecclesiastes, where the voice of the preacher is heard, and into the conservatory of Sharon and the lily of the valley where sweet spices filled and perfumed my life.

I entered the business office of Proverbs and on into the observatory of the prophets where I saw telescopes of various sizes pointing to far-off events, concentrating on the bright and morning star which was to rise above the moonlit hills of Judea for our salvation and redemption.

I entered the audience room of the King of Kings, catching a vision written by Matthew, Mark, Luke and John. Thence into the correspondence room with Paul, Peter, James and John writing their epistles.

I stepped into the throne room of Revelation where tower the glittering peaks, where sits the King of Kings upon His throne of glory with the healing of the nations in His hand, and I cried out:

"All hail the power of Jesus' Name,
Let angels prostrate fall;
Bring forth the royal diadem,
And crown Him Lord of all."

VIII. Happiness Is Knowing the Joy of Service

Here is a man who accepts Christ, is baptized and becomes a member of the church. But he stops right there, he goes no farther. I would not call him a happy Christian. Now we know that not every man can teach a class or sing a solo or preach a sermon, but every Christian can find something to do for the Lord. A man once told me that he couldn't serve the Lord in a job where he had to work with a group of colored men in a turpentine camp. But I tell you that you can serve Him anywhere. Don Moomaw, the great football player, said, "I want to be an All-American for Christ." So he served Christ as he played football and he became a strong witness for Christ. Bobby Richardson, of the New York Yankees, signed a baseball contract when he was eighteen years of age. He went to training camp but was soon lonely and homesick. A letter came from his high school coach saying, "Stay where you are and stay there as a Christian." He stayed and in the baseball write-ups about the champion Yankees you can read often of his Christian activities on the field and off. Alvin Dark was an All-American athlete at Louisiana State. He is now manager of the San Francisco Giant baseball team. When he began his baseball career he did not leave Christianity behind. He testifies often for the Lord. He tells how God has blessed him in his tithing.

Ty Cobb, "the Georgia Peach," was the greatest all-time baseball player in America. He broke all of the records. He died in 1961. Just before he died he accepted Christ. Then he sent a word to baseball players everywhere. He said, "Tell the boys that I am sorry it was the last part of the ninth inning that I came to know Christ. I wish I had taken Him as my Saviour in the first half of the first." Don't let it be that way with you. Don't wait until the end of life before you realize that you ought to serve God. Come now and find happiness in giving Him your very best service.

IX. HAPPINESS IS KNOWING THAT YOU HAVE A HOME
AWAITING YOU AT THE END OF THE WAY

Some people who were here a year ago are gone now.
Some of us who are here now will not be living a year from
now. But if you know Christ all is well. You have a home
waiting for you at the end of the way. Of course, we want
to live. All of us look forward to the completion of our future plans and the fulfillment of our earthly dreams. But
God has planned far better things for us over there than
we can ever enjoy here.

Robert Louis Stevenson was seriously ill most of his
life. But he kept on working and giving the world some of
its greatest literature. Instead of giving up, he took these
words as his motto: "Cling to what is left. Make the best
of what remains." I don't know how much longer you and
I have, but I would like to give you some similar advice.
Cling to God and give Him your best service the balance
of your days.

Dr. B. H. Carroll was a great preacher of the Southwest.
When he was converted he prayed this prayer:

Write Thy name on my head
That I may think for Thee;
Write Thy name on my lips
That I may speak for Thee;
Write Thy name on my feet
That I may walk with and for Thee;
Write Thy name on my hands
That I may work with and for Thee;
Write Thy name on my ears
That I may listen for Thee;
Write Thy name on my heart
That I may love Thee;
Write Thy name on my shoulders
That I may bear loads for Thee;
Write Thy name on my eyes
That I may see for Thee;
Write Thy name all over me
That I may be wholly Thine —
always and everywhere.

God help us to give our very best to Him in all the days to come. Then when we reach the land beyond the sunset we will know a happiness which passes all understanding.

4

Payday

Ecclesiastes 12:13, 14

All of us are interested in payday. The girl who makes $25.00 a week looks forward to that day. Often she has to live on simple fare for a day or two before that time. The man who makes $100,000 per year looks forward to payday. He needs this money for heavy expenses. The retired couple watches the mail for their pension. They need it for the necessities of life. The law of life is that if a man works for another he is supposed to get payment for that work. If you work for someone a month and he refuses to pay you, you can call down the law upon him.

The same law of payment applies in the spiritual realm. God also pays off. He pays off in two places, here and hereafter. He pays off in two ways. If you serve sin, He will pay off with punishment. If you serve Him, He will pay off with a reward. Judgment is one of the biggest topics in the Bible. Paul said to that group of intellectuals at Athens, "And the times of this ignorance God winked at; but now commandeth all men everywhere to repent. Because He hath appointed a day, in the which He will judge the world in righteousness by that man whom He hath ordained; whereof He hath given assurance unto all men, in that He hath raised Him from the dead." God guaranteed judgment when He raised Him from the dead.

Listen to the words of the tenderhearted Jesus, "And thou, Capernaum, which art exalted unto heaven, shalt be brought down to hell; for if the mighty works, which have been done in thee, had been done in Sodom, it would have remained until this day. But I say unto you, that it shall be more tolerable for the land of Sodom in the day of judgment, than for thee." Christ is saying here that Sodom was a wicked city, but that those who know about Christ and reject Him will suffer more at the judgment than the people of Sodom.

Matthew 12:36 says, "But I say unto you, that every idle word that men shall speak, they shall give account thereof in the day of judgment." In Ecclesiastes 11:9 we hear the inspired writer saying, "Rejoice, O young man, in thy youth; and let thy heart cheer thee in the days of thy youth, and walk in the ways of thine heart, and in the sight of thine eyes: but know thou, that for all these things God will bring thee into judgment." The Bible is telling us that we can go ahead and live as we please, but that always we must remember that one day we will have to face God and give an account of these lives.

God does not always wait until the end of life to pay off. We often have to face judgment right here. There is an old saying that "a young man must sow his wild oats." If he does, he is going to reap the harvest. "Be not deceived, God is not mocked, for whatsoever a man soweth that shall he also reap." This text was written primarily to Christians. God is saying, "Sins must be paid for, both here and hereafter."

I. Everything About Calvary Is a Picture of Judgment

Look at the cross and you will see the holy Son of God dying there. Why is He hanging there, why is He suffering, why is He dying? Never did He commit a sin, never did He have an evil thought. He is dying there in judgment. He is paying for your sins and mine. The Bible tells us that He was "made sin" for us. He did not sin, but He was made sin for us. All of our sins and the sins of the world were on Him. Sin had to be punished and God's wrath fell upon Him instead of us.

He said on one occasion, "As Moses lifted up the serpent in the wilderness, so must the Son of Man be lifted up: that whosoever believeth in Him should not perish, but have eternal life." You remember how the Israelites were bitten by the fiery serpents. This meant certain death. There was absolutely no human remedy available, but Moses was told by the Lord to put a brazen serpent on a pole in the center of the camp. Those who looked to that serpent were healed. So today men are bitten by the serpent of sin. There is no human remedy for their malady. But God has provided a divine remedy. He gave His Son. That Son was lifted up on a cross and those who look to Him in faith are saved.

But how could a serpent be a type of Christ? All through the Bible the serpent is a type of sin and Satan. The serpent came into Eden and deceived Adam and Eve. He is spoken of as "that old serpent, the devil." Well, there is only one time when the serpent was a type of Christ. In the Old Testament brass was the symbol of judgment. So this serpent, representing sin and being made of brass, represents sin unto judgment. So as we look at Christ on the cross, we see that He is taking the sinner's place. We see judgment falling upon Him.

There were three hours of darkness while He hung on the cross. This is also a picture of judgment. We are told that in the judgment those who have rejected Christ will be cast into outer darkness. So this darkness fell upon the earth while He hung upon the cross. This is simply a picture of the awful darkness which will surround sinners in their eternal doom.

We are told also that Christ was made a curse for us when He hung on the cross. Just think of it. He was the finest person who ever lived. He opened blind eyes, He caused the lame to walk, He cast out devils, He healed the sick. His every touch was tender and blessed. Think of One like that being made an accursed thing. But He bore it all for you and me.

Even the soil of this earth is under a curse because of
sin. The Bible tells us that this is the reason we have thorns.
Well, they pressed a crown of thorns upon His brow. What
does this tell us? It tells us that Jesus is being made a curse
for us. Oh, how much He was willing to bear, all because
He loved us so much.

Here is another picture of judgment at Calvary. He
cried out, "My God, my God, why hast Thou forsaken Me?"
This was the only time He ever addressed the Heavenly
Father as "God." Heretofore He had always called Him
"Father." Now as He hangs on the cross, He does not bear
the relationhip of a son. For the time being, because our
sin is on Him, this is the cry of a sinner to his God. He was
forsaken because He was bearing our sin in His own body
on the tree. God's pure eyes could not look upon that sight.
This is a picture of a lost sinner in hell. He will be absolutely
forsaken of God. Today he breathes God's free air, he en-
joys all the blessings of God. But then he will be cut off
from God forever.

So we see that Calvary is the picture of judgment, the
judgment which fell on Jesus because of our sin. This was
Jesus' payday. He didn't deserve it, but He bore it all for us.

II. Now Look at the Christian's Payday

First, we think of the payday for his sins. A Christian
does sin after he has been saved. What is he to do about it?
Some people think that he is lost and will have to be saved
again. No, as we are born only once, so we are born again
only once. We are saved only once. What, then, does God
do with a Christian when he sins? Does He throw him out?
Does He disown him? Does He send him to hell? No. In
the eighty-ninth Psalm He says, "Then will I visit their
transgressions with the rod, and their iniquity with stripes.
Nevertheless my loving kindness will I not utterly take
from him, nor suffer my faithfulness to fail." In Hebrews
12, He says, "My son, despise not thou the chastening of the

Lord, nor faint when thou art rebuked of Him: for whom the Lord loveth He chasteneth, and scourgeth every son whom He receiveth. If ye endure chastening, God dealeth with you as with sons; for what son is he whom the father chasteneth not? But if ye be without chastisement, whereof all are partakers, then are ye bastards, and not sons." We are simply being told here that if the children of God sin, God will punish them or chastise them right now. That chastisement will be for their own good.

A certain preacher delivered a sermon on how God chastises and corrects His children. A fashionable lady came up at the close of the sermon, elegantly dressed and with diamonds sparkling on her hands. She said to the preacher, "I don't believe a word you have preached tonight." The preacher said, "That's strange. I got it out of the Bible." Then the lady said, "You talked about God chastising His children. I do all the things you talked about. I drink, I smoke, I play cards, I give cocktail parties. I have been a member of the church for thirty-five years, but God doesn't chastise me." The preacher opened his Bible and read, "But if ye be without chastisement, whereof all are partakers, ye are not sons, but bastards." The woman went away angry. But it wasn't the preacher who said this, it was God. You may be a church member, but if you run after the world and chase after sin and God doesn't lay the rod on you, then you may know that you are not His child.

When you see your neighbor's children doing wrong, you do not punish them. But when your own children do wrong, you punish them. Well, God sees the devil's children in sin and He doesn't chastise them. He saves that for the punishment of hell. But when He sees His own children doing wrong, He chastises them because He loves them. I know that my father loved me, because he chastised me often and tried to make something out of me. We know that God loves us when He chastises us and seeks to make us what we ought to be.

In writing to the church at Corinth Paul pointed out the sin among them. He said that some of them were sick and some had died simply because they had not cleaned the sins out of the church. In our present-day churches there are some who criticize and find fault and hold back the work and God sometimes takes them away to heaven. Oh, listen, when God speaks He means it. A Christian can't get away with sin. He will not send you to hell if you are His child, but He will not let your sin go unpunished. Sometimes we go along without a cloud in the sky and suddenly something happens to hurt us. Then we look back and say, "I know why this has come. I remember my sin and now God is punishing me."

But here is a wonderful thing. In I Corinthians 11:31 we read, "For if we would judge ourselves, we should not be judged." What does this mean? I believe it means that if we sin and then sit in judgment upon ourselves, hating ourselves for what we have done, and if we confess our sin and get it out of our lives, we will then escape the rod of God. That's the way it is in a family. One day a boy does something wrong and immediately realizes it. He runs to his father and in tears he confesses his wrong and asks his father to forgive him. The father is not then likely to punish him. But if that boy goes his way, continually doing wrong, then when the father catches him he will surely use the rod on him. It is the same way with God. So if you have something wrong in your life, hurry and confess it. Turn away from it lest your punishment be severe.

Next let's think of the Christian's payday for his works. God is mighty wonderful! He saves you, then He promises to pay off for the work that you do in His Name. Matthew 16:27 — "For the Son of Man shall come in the glory of His Father with His angels: and then He shall reward every man according to his works." Here is the Bible order of events. Christ will come in the air, and take up to be with Him all Christians, both dead and living. He will then set up the Judgment Seat. This will not be a throne of condemnation but a place of reward. He will judge all the works that we have done for Him and reward us accordingly. The Bible teaches us that if these works have been for our own glory, they will be burned up, even though you will be saved. But if our works are for God's glory, then He will give us a rich reward. Some of you teach a Sunday school class, or you serve in some department of our church life. Are you serving for your own glory or for God's glory? Some of you sing in the choir, some of you pay your tithe, you are faithful to every service. Every Christian ought to be faithful and active and generous, but all of it should be for the glory of God.

Now what about some people who have been saved and are content to stop right there. They are not faithful to the church, they are not growing in grace, they are not serving the Lord, they are not giving as they should. If they have been really born again, they will go to heaven all right, but there will be no reward for them. All their works will be burned up. When we remember that God loved us and that Christ died to keep us out of hell and that He is taking us to heaven, how can we help but want to give Him the best of our lives?

In *Pilgrim's Progress* Christian has seen Christ and has been gloriously saved. How does he feel? We hear him saying, "If I had a thousand gallons of blood in my body, I would want to pour out every drop for Him." How cold is much of our love in comparison to the great love of Christ.

In the Bible a crown is a picture or symbol of reward. The Bible mentions several crowns which will be given to certain people at the Judgment Seat. There is the soul-winner's crown. It is a crown of rejoicing. If you have won a single soul to Christ, you will receive this crown at the Judgment Seat. . . . Then there is the crown of life which is given for faithfulness. Revelation 2:10 -- "Be thou faithful unto death and I will give thee a crown of life." This crown is not promised to the Christians who take it easy, to those who serve God for a while and then serve the devil for a while. It is for those who are faithful to the last step of the way.

Then there is the crown of glory for the true preachers of the Gospel. I don't deserve any credit for it, but I believe that I have been true to the Gospel. I have tried to preach the truth of the Bible from Genesis to Revelation. I have never doubted any of it. However, I believe that this crown is not only for preachers, but for the faithful teachers of the Word of God. Then there is the crown of righteousness for those who love the appearing of Christ. Can you honestly say that you would love to have Jesus return? You can't say this unless your life is in good shape. Unless you are clean in your life and busy in His service, you don't want Him to come at this time. The only ones who love His appearing are those who love Him and who are doing their best for Him.

Then there is the incorruptible crown. Paul speaks of the man who is running a race. He says that this crown is not for the man who runs poorly, but for the one who throws aside every hindrance and strives to win. Many of you are going to heaven simply because of the grace of God. You are loaded down with too many worldly things. Your clubs, your lodges, your social life, many earthly things are holding you down so that you can't run a good race. If you want heaven to mean the most to you, if you want to please Christ the most, if you want to live a happier life, if you want to mean more to others, then pick up all of these worldly things and throw them overboard for Jesus' sake.

I have heard so many people say, "I have so many things to do that I will have to give up some of my church work." Some of them say, "I have so many worldly obligations that I can't afford to tithe." Oh, I wish that you would say to the world, "I am going to give you up so that I will have more time for my Lord. I am going to give up some of my worldly obligations so that I can support God's work as I should." You will never know true happiness until you arrive at that point.

Yes, there is a payday for the Christian. There is a payday because he has sinned. There is a payday if he has lived for Christ. And suppose you do win a crown, what are you going to do with it? Surely you will want to kneel down at Jesus' feet and give it all to Him. He is the One who deserves it all. He is the One who has saved you and brought you home.

III. THE SINNER'S PAYDAY

The man who goes through life without Christ will one day stand before the Great White Throne Judgment. The One who died for you will be sitting on that throne. He will judge you out of the things written in His books. Your punishment will be set for all of eternity. Remember that only the unsaved will be at the Great White Throne Judgment. Remember also that this is not a judgment to determine whether you are saved or lost. The man who appears there is already lost because he has rejected Christ. There is no second chance for him. His punishment is set. We don't know the extent of that punishment, but we do know that the Bible says that sinners will be tormented day and night forever and ever.

Today when you talk to some men about salvation, they begin to tell you about their good lives and their good deeds. Jesus said it would be the same way when they faced Him. Matthew 7:21-23—"Not every one that saith unto me, Lord, Lord, shall enter into the kingdom of heaven; but he that doeth the will of my Father which is in heaven. Many will say to me in that day, Lord, Lord, have we not prophesied in thy name? and in thy name have cast out devils? and in thy name done many wonderful works? And then will I profess unto them, I never knew you: depart from me, ye that work iniquity."

Yes, when these people face the Lord they will say,

"Lord, look what I did. You ought to let me into heaven."
Then God will reach up for the Book of Life and show them
that their names have not been written there. For He says
in Revelation 20:15—"And whosoever was not found written
in the book of life was cast into the lake of fire." Do you
want your names written there? You will not get them there
by trusting in your own good deeds and gifts, but by coming to God as a penitent sinner and trusting Jesus Christ
as your personal Saviour.

In 1927 a young man and his best girl were walking
down the street in a Florida city. They were deeply in love.
They stopped in front of a large beautiful house. The young
man said, "Maybe some day we will have a house like that."
The street had just been freshly paved and he took a stick
and scratched their initials in the concrete. They were married soon after that. They worked hard. They lived in small
houses, but they kept on dreaming about that larger house.
Just a few months ago they bought that house and moved
in. Their initials were still there, hardened in the concrete.
It was a happy day for them when they moved into their
dream house.

It is sweet to own the house that you have dreamed
about. It is sweeter to have a title to the eternal home. Jesus
said, "I go to prepare a place for you." That place will be
yours only if you take Him as your Saviour. Yes, payday
is coming some day. What will it be for you? Will it be
a time of sorrow and bitter remorse? Or will it be a time
of rejoicing as the Lord rewards you in heaven? The decision is up to you.

5

Physicians with No Healing Power

Mark 5:24-34

Jesus never turned down anyone who was in need. He always gave Himself gladly and freely for others. In the story in our text we find Him near the sea. The crowds are following Him. It seems that they would never leave Him. Then a man named Jairus came and fell at His feet, crying out, "Lord, I am in trouble. My little girl is sick. I am afraid that she is dying and it is breaking my heart. I just don't feel that I can give her up. Please come and lay your hand upon her and I am sure she will be healed." Jesus was touched by this request and said to the man, "I will help you. Let us go to your house." So they started out to Jairus' house with the crowd following them.

But Jairus was not the only one in trouble. There was a woman in the crowd who had been sick for twelve years. She had gone to one doctor after another and there had been no cure for her. She felt that Jesus could help her, but she was too timid to make a direct approach. She just stole up close to Him and touched the hem of His garment. Jesus felt the power go out of Him and He said, "Who touched my clothes?" The disciples said, "Lord, there is a great crowd here. Why do you ask who touched you?" Then Jesus said, "But I felt the power go out of me and I know that someone touched me who was in need." Of course, He knew who it was. He looked straight at the woman and she came and fell at His feet. She poured out her heart to Him, and He said, "Daughter, thy faith hath made thee whole. Go in peace." Then the woman went

49

away rejoicing. Jesus had done more for her than all of the doctors.

This is the story of a great faith and a great Saviour. Let us, with the help of the Holy Spirit, learn some great lessons from this story.

I. THIS WOMAN WAS SICK

For twelve long years she had suffered. At the beginning of each year she must have said, "Maybe this year I will be better." On the first of each month she must have said. "Certainly this will be a good month for me." But healing never came. This is a picture of the lost sinner. This is a picture of the man who needs the touch of God. A man over in India took a cup of water out of the sacred Ganges River and showed it to some natives under a microscope. When they saw all the germs swimming around in the water they broke the microscope. They did not want to look facts in the face. The sinner is like that. The Bible tells him that he is a sinner. His conscience tells him the same. But he doesn't listen. He is sick in his sin.

The state of Georgia once had a great senator named Benjamin H. Hill. One day a little article in the daily paper said, "Senator Hill is having a little trouble with his tongue. The trouble came from a fractured tooth." Later an operation was performed and he was pronounced to be all right. But later on there was another operation performed in Philadelphia. They found that the senator had cancer and the paper stated, "The doctors hope that they got all of the cancer and that the senator will soon be well again." A few months later there was another item on the front page of the Atlanta paper. It read, "The grandest procession that ever moved through Atlanta yesterday followed the body of Senator Benjamin H. Hill to the cemetery." It was just a little thing, but it led to his death. Sin starts in a little way but it leads to death and hell.

A preacher friend of mine was pastor of a large church. One day a girl in sin came to him for help. The preacher and his wife took this girl into their home and gave her privacy and love. They found out that she was a preacher's daughter from another part of the state. The pastor wired for this preacher father to come and he came, expecting to be recommended to another church. The pastor told the old preacher the story of the girl's trouble, and then said to him, "My wife and I are going out for a little ride now and we will leave you and your daughter alone." When he returned he found the old preacher lying on the bed and his daughter trying to comfort him. When he came in, the old preacher said, "Oh, Dr. Owen, it hurts so, it hurts so." Sin always hurts. It hurts the sinner and it hurts all of those who are connected with him. But every sinner is afflicted with the same disease.

II. This Woman Tried Many Physicians

Mark says that she "suffered many things of many physicians." You know how it is. When you catch a cold everybody has a remedy. Some years ago I had a touch of poison ivy on my face. Everybody told me what to do about it. If I had used all of the remedies it would have killed me. Now Luke tells the same story, even though he was a doctor himself. He said that she had spent all of her money paying doctor bills. I believe that we ought always to pay the doctor. Sometimes he is the last one to be paid. You can never tell when you are going to need him. You ought to keep everything straight between you and your doctor, then you won't be embarrassed when you have to call him in the middle of the night.

Now as these doctors were helpless in the face of this woman's disease, so the worldly spiritual physicians are helpless in the face of the disease called sin. Let us look at some of them.

1. *There is Dr Atheist.* He examines the patient and says, "Don't worry. There is no God, there is no hereafter. You need not be troubled about the future." Then he goes

his way and the poor sinner must say, "He didn't help me. He didn't heal my disease. My heart is still aching, my sin still condemns me."

A certain man ran down to the dock and leaped into the water. Someone threw him a rope but he thrust it aside. They pulled the rope in and threw it to him again. Again he pushed it aside. The man with the rope said, "That man must be crazy." And he was crazy. He had escaped from an insane asylum and he went down to his death. The atheist is like that. He is drowning in sin. You throw him the rope of the Gospel and he thrusts it aside. Because of this he goes down to death. Dr. Atheist cannot help you. He will simply leave you floundering in your sin.

2. *There is Dr. Agnostic.* The atheist says, "There is no God." The agnostic says, "I don't know whether there is a God or not." Dr. Agnostic examines the patient and says, "No man knows if there is a God or whether there is a future life or whether a man has a soul." When he goes away the poor sinner still must say, "He did not help me. My sin is still a burden upon me."

A doctor who was an agnostic said to a preacher, "Can you see a soul?" The preacher answered, "No." Then the doctor said, "Can you hear a soul? Can you taste a soul? Can you smell a soul?" The preacher answered, "No," to all of these questions. Then the doctor said, "Can you feel the soul?" And the preacher answered, "Yes." "All right," said the doctor, "by the majority of four senses to one I have proved to you that there is no such thing as a soul." Then the preacher said, "Can you see a pain? Can you hear a pain? Can you taste a pain? Can you smell a pain?" And the doctor answered, "No." Then the preacher asked, "Can you feel a pain?" Of course the doctor answered, "Yes." Then the preacher said, "I have proved by a majority of four senses to one that there is no such thing as a pain. But you know that pain exists and I know that the soul exists."

The agnostic says, "I don't know anything about God

and the soul and eternal life." Paul says, "For I know whom I have believed, and am persuaded that he is able to keep that which I have committed unto him against that day."

3. *There is Dr. No Hell.* This doctor says, "Don't worry, there is no such place as hell. There is no punishment for the sinner. God is merciful and He will not punish you." When this doctor goes his way this poor sinner cries out, "He did not help me. My sin is convicting me and I am in hell now."

We don't accept the doctrine of hell because we delight in it, but because it is in the Bible. It is a scriptural fact. All of your doubts won't fill the pit or block the gate. Suppose that I saw you riding down the road at a speed of seventy-five miles per hour and I knew that a great precipice was looming up before you and you were headed for death. Wouldn't I be merciful to warn you and to save you from death? Oh, sinner, there is nothing ahead of you at the end of the way but suffering and hell. Let me warn you to flee to Christ and away from the wrath to come.

4. *There is Dr. Good Enough.* He says to the sinner, "Don't worry about your sins. You are a good man. You are honest. You don't harm anyone. You pay your debts. You are good enough." When he goes away the poor sinner says, "He didn't help me. I know that I am not good. I know that I have sinned against God."

You can always tell when a man is far away from God. He talks about how good he is. The nearer a man is to God, the more easily does he see his own sin. When Isaiah saw God he cried out, "Woe is me. I am a man of unclean lips." When Peter saw the Lord he cried out, "Depart from me, for I am a sinful man." No man is ever good enough to be saved. "By grace are ye saved through faith, and that not of yourselves, it is the gift of God: not of works, lest any man should boast." Let us send Dr. Good Enough away, he can never help us.

5. *There is Dr. Do Better.* He says to the sinner, "I know that you are bad, but just do better in the future and everything will be all right." When he goes his way the poor sinner says, "I will try to do better, but that will not blot out my guilty past. I am a sinner, what must I do?"

Here is a man who is trusted by a business firm. Then he steals $100,000 from them. The management tells him that he must do better in the future. "All right," says the man, "the next time I will just take $50,000." No, that doesn't clear things up. That man is punished for what he has done in the past. So if there is sin in your heart, you can't clear things up by saying, "I am not going to sin as much in the future as I have in the past." Even if you could live a perfect life from now until the day you die, that would not clear up the past. Let us send Dr. Do Better away.

6. *The Great Physician is the only One who can help us.* These other doctors are quacks. He alone has the remedy for sin. He examines you and says, "You've sinned and you are lost. But I love you and I will save you. I went to the cross for that purpose. So repent of your sin and put your trust in Me. Him that cometh to Me, I will in no wise cast out. Come now and let us reason together, though your sins be as scarlet, they shall be as white as snow."

Then the sinner shouts, "That's the doctor for me. I will take the remedy. I know that He will save me and give me peace." This is what the woman did. Jesus not only healed her, but He gave her the peace that only He can give.

III. This Woman Had Faith

1. *It was a timid faith.* She did not speak out, she just slipped up and touched the hem of his garment. Do you see the humility in this? Great souls are not always loud. There are some who are never able to speak in public, but deep down in their hearts they have a great faith and a great love for Jesus. Some of the greatest Christians on earth are the quiet ones.

2. *It was a great faith.* She said, "If I may touch but
His clothes, I shall be whole." Think of it! This woman
had been going to doctors for twelve years and they had
not helped her. Then when she saw Jesus she believed
that a simple touch would make her whole. Oh, woman,
great is thy faith! We are never saved without some effort.
If this woman had stayed back in the crowd she never would
have been cured. Jesus has the remedy for your sin. Why
not step up and take it?

The world has been blessed by women of great faith.
William Booth had a great church in the city of London.
He began to preach to the poor people in the slums and
the high authorities in the church threatened to take his
position away from him if he didn't quit going down among
these poor people and preaching. When he wavered in
his faith, his mother said to him, "It doesn't matter what
happens to you. You must never give up this ministry for
the poor." Out of that faith was born the Salvation Army.

3. *It was a faith based upon little knowledge.* This
woman did not know as much about Jesus as we do. She
just knew two things. She knew that she was sick and that
Christ could heal her. This is all you need to know. You
are a sinner and Christ can save you. You don't have to
know about all the doctrines of the faith. You don't have
to know a large number of scripture verses. You don't have
to know all about prophecy. You just need to know two
things. You need to know that you are lost and that Christ
can save you.

Dr. Luther Little was for many years pastor of the
First Baptist Church of Charlotte, North Carolina. He was
holding a meeting in a certain place and one day in the
lobby of his hotel he invited a traveling man to come to the
services. This man said, "Doctor, I will come to church if
you will answer three questions for me. Where did Cain
get his wife? Who was Melchizedek? What is the immacu-
late conception?" Dr. Little looked the man straight in the

eye and said, "You will be in hell ten thousand years before you find the answers to these questions." The man saw the folly of his thinking, began to go to church and was soon converted. You don't need the hard questions answered as much as you need to repent of your sins and trust Christ as your Saviour.

IV. This Woman Was Made Whole

When she touched the hem of His garment, the power flowed out from Him and she was healed. So when we touch Him by faith His saving power flows down to us. When you are sick you go to a reputable physician and you say, "Doctor, my case is in your hands." Jesus has the reputation for saving souls. Come and put your case in His hands.

Now this woman's greatest joy came when she confessed Christ. When she was healed that was a secret blessing. When she made her confession the blessing overflowed. Christ says that if we confess Him before men, He will confess us before the Father which is in heaven. This woman confessed Him and now we hear Him saying, "Daughter, thy faith hath made thee whole. Go in peace." The Bible says, "For with the heart man believeth unto righteousness; and with the mouth confession is made unto salvation." A man joined the church of which I was pastor one Sunday morning, and later he said to me, "Three weeks ago I decided for Christ. But it was when I came to confess Him that the real joy entered my soul."

Gypsy Smith's father lived in a tent with his five children. His wife was dead. He had been converted to Christ and he did the best he could to bring up his children in a Christian manner. Each night he prayed and sang with them. As their fresh young voices rang out in the night air, the neighbors and passers-by could hear them. One woman, upon hearing the singing, came under deep conviction for sin. She said to herself, "That poor gypsy and his children are singing and praying in the tent yonder. I have been greatly blessed, but I never pray." When her husband came home from work he said to her, "Are you sick?" When she made no answer her husband sent for a doctor who gave her something to quiet her nerves. As soon as the doctor left the woman sent for the gypsy and said, "I have heard you and your children singing and praying. Will you pray for me? Will you tell me how to be saved?" He prayed for her and soon she was rejoicing in Christ.

The next morning the doctor came to see her again and when he entered the room the woman shouted, "Doctor, I have found Him! I have found Him!" "My poor soul," said the doctor, "whom have you found?" And she replied, "I have found the One that my poor soul has been hungry for. I have found Jesus." "Well," said the doctor, "you don't need me. You have found the greatest Physician in the world."

Yes, my friends, He is just exactly that. He is what the world needs. He is what you need. Come and touch Him and let His blessings flow into your soul today.

6

Know the Real Joy of Good Living

II Timothy 4:1-8

A certain brewery uses this slogan in advertising their beer: *"Know the Real Joy of Good Living."* They claim that if you learn how to drink their beer you will really be living. So they say that, "Beer Belongs." Their ads show a picture of a man coming home in the evening and his wife has the beer ready for him. They picture some company sitting at the dinner table and the beer is on the table. They picture a barbecue in the backyard with everyone drinking beer. They picture a group gathered after a football game where the beer is passed around. This is their idea of good living, but it is different from God's idea.

There is a joke about a rich Texan who was asked when he lay dying if he had any last requests to make. He said, "Yes, when I die, bury me in my gold Cadillac." So when he died they put him in his gold Cadillac and lowered the car into a big hole. A certain man who came to the funeral said, "Man, that's real living!" Yes, wealth and affluence is to some people the right idea of good living.

To others service is the real secret of good living. A young doctor gave up a wealthy practice and went abroad as a medical missionary. His father visited him and saw him perform several difficult operations. One of these operations lasted several hours. His father asked him, "How much would you get for that operation in the United States?" The young doctor replied, "I would probably receive $1,000 for it there. Here I get nothing but the knowledge that I have helped someone. But man, that's real living!" Now who is right? The beer company or the Christian doctor?

I. What Is Good Living?

1. *Good living involves commitment to Christ.* A man may have fine health, a good job, a nice family and a lovely home and yet never come face to face with Jesus Christ in an experience of saving grace. That is not living, that is just existing. A certain man was saved when he was eighty years of age. When he was eighty-four years of age one of his grandchildren asked him how old he was. He said that he was only four years of age. He said, "I spent eighty years in the service of Satan. I have known Christ only four years. Therefore I say that I am only four years of age. I never really and truly began to live until I met Jesus."

You are headed for eternity. None of us can expect more than just a few more years, then we will go out to face God. If you know Christ you are really living here and you are hurrying on toward eternal life. If you don't know Jesus Christ, your life lacks the best things here and you are heading toward eternal death. The most important thing in life is to get ready for life and death by committing yourself to Christ. The Bible says in Romans 10:9-11—"That if thou shalt confess with thy mouth the Lord Jesus, and shalt believe in thine heart that God hath raised him from the dead, thou shalt be saved. For with the heart man believeth unto righteousness; and with the mouth confession is made unto salvation. For the scripture saith, Whosoever believeth on him shall not be ashamed." When you commit yourself to Christ, you have planted your feet on the road to good living.

2. *Good living involves a vital church connection.* By this I don't mean that you simply have your name on a church roll book. You will have a connection that means something. It means faithfulness, it means service, it mean fellowship. You can go to any church roll and find the names of people who have not been inside the church for many years. They

have no vital church connection. There is no real life there. The church means nothing to them and they mean nothing to the church. When I remember that Christ loved the church and died for it and when I remember that He established local churches here for us to serve through, I would be ashamed if I allowed my Christian life to be simply a name on a book. Where did you learn about Christ and salvation? It was either in a church or through someone or some institution which was given this knowledge by the church. If the church had not cradled the Gospel and brought it down to us, we would be lost in the darkness of sin. Only eternity can reveal what the Christian churches have meant to the world. Our city would be a place like hell if it did not have in it the influence of the church.

3. *Good living involves a separation from the world.* You can't commit yourself to Christ and join the church and then live a worldly life and call it good living. We must be in the world but we don't have to be of the world. We don't have to sink down to the level of worldlings.

At one time Dr. M. A. Jenkins was pastor of a church in Macon, Georgia. One day the operator of the biggest saloon and gambling den in the city came to church. He came under conviction for sin and told the preacher that he wanted to talk to him. The preacher went out to see him the next day and told him about Christ. He prayed with him and left some scripture passages for him to study. The next morning this man called Dr. Jenkins and said, "At one o'clock this morning I was reading the scripture that you left me. The light of God flooded my soul. I gave my heart to Christ and I am going to live for Him." The next Sunday Dr. Jenkins baptized the man and his wife. Sometime later as he passed this man's house he saw a truck hauling out some mahogany furniture. Dr. Jenkins went in and asked the reason for this. The man replied, "I made my money selling liquor and I have observed that money made in that way always leaves a curse. I am getting rid of everything that I bought with liquor money so that it won't bring a curse upon me and my children." On another day Dr. Jenkins met this man and he was all smiles. He said, "A big brewer came to me and said, 'John, quit that blankety-blank preacher and throw in with me and I will make you rich. I will set you up in a wonderful business and make you the best saloon man in town.'" Dr. Jenkins asked, "What did you tell him?" And the man replied, "I told him that the blankety-blank preacher was my kind now. I told him that I had turned from my sins and was on the way to heaven. I told him that Christ was now my Saviour and that by the grace of God I was through with the work of the devil forever."

Yes, it's good living when you can say, "I am through with the old life and I am now living for Jesus Christ."

4. *Good living involves walking with God.* You can't walk with Him unless you are going His way. His way is not the way of Mr. Schlitz or Falstaff or Budweiser or any other questionable thing. Several years ago I attended church one morning in a Florida city. Some seats were reserved for the American Legion. A large group of these men attended church that morning and their leader said, "Our attendance at church is a part of our back-to-God movement. We attend church in a body once each month." After the service that morning the preacher showed me a sign on a bar two blocks from the church. The sign read, "American Legion Bar." On one hand they were talking about "Back to God." On the other hand they were selling the thing that God is against. They were not walking with God. When you walk with God you walk in a clean pathway.

5. *Good living includes communion with God.* This means prayer and Bible study. In prayer we talk to God, in Bible study God talks to us.

And He walks with me and He talks with me,
And He tells me I am His own,
And the joys we share as we tarry there,
None other has ever known.

6. *Good living includes serving God.* During the days of slavery a girl was being sold on the auction block. A man came along who was touched with her plight and bought her. As he led her away she said to herself, "Yes, he bought me so that he could use me as he would an animal." When they had gone some distance from the crowd he said to the girl, "You can go free now. I bought you to set you free." She didn't understand this for a moment, so he repeated his statement. The tears rolled down her cheeks and she fell at his feet, saying, "Oh, master, I want to serve you the rest of my life."

There was a time when Satan had us in his power and he was taking us to hell. But Jesus went to Calvary and bought us for His very own. He has set us free from judgment and hell. We ought to fall at His feet and cry out, "Master, I will serve You as long as I live." That is one of the joys of good living.

7. *Good living implies co-operation with God in a world-wide task.* God wants you to do something for your next-door neighbor, but that is not all. He wants you to help everyone who does not know Christ. He may call some of you to serve on a full-time basis. He calls everyone of us to give our tithe to support His work. The word "rob" is a hard word. You wouldn't rob a bank, you wouldn't break into a house. But God says that men are robbing Him by not bringing His tithe into His storehouse. The consecrated Christian gets no joy out of taking God's money and using it for himself. That is not good living. The nominal Christian sees no harm in doing this. He doesn't care.

God's work is the biggest and most important work in the world. It will last when the stars have died out and the world is no more. Are you having a vital part in it?

Only one life, 'twill soon be past,
Only what's done for Christ will last.

Now these things constitute good living. You will notice that Christ is in the center of it all.

II. LET US LOOK AT THE JOY FOUND IN THIS GOOD LIVING

1. *You know that your sins are forgiven.* This happened when you committed yourself to Christ.

Did you know that one of the best men in the Bible was one of the greatest sinners on a particular occasion? David was "a man after God's own heart." Yet the time came when he broke four of the ten commandments at one time. He coveted. He committed adultery. He put flesh before God. He murdered. That is a black record, isn't it? But because he was "a man after God's own heart," he came to God in repentance and God graciously forgave him. Then he wrote the words, "Blessed is the man whose iniquity is forgiven, whose transgression is covered." And the God who forgave David's great sin will also forgive yours. Isn't that a real joy of good living?

2. *You know that you have someone to help you along life's way.* Jesus said before He left the earth, "I will not leave you as orphans. I will not leave you comfortless. I will send you my Holy Spirit." And the minute you commit yourself to Christ the Holy Spirit comes to dwell in your heart. What would you do when sorrow comes and the heart is breaking if you could not hear Him say, "Let not your heart be troubled"? What would you do when it seems that the world has forsaken you if you could not hear Him say, "I will never leave you nor forsake you"? What would you do when friends turn their backs upon you if you could not hear Him whisper, "There is a friend that sticketh closer than a brother"? What would you do when the responsibilities of life crowd in upon you if you could not hear Him say, "You can do all things through Christ which strengtheneth you"? What would you do in

the time of need, if you could not hear Him say, "My God shall supply every need of yours"?

In Bunyan's *Pilgrim's Progress* Christian comes to a chasm where one misstep will mean death. Then a pathway opened up before him and he heard a voice saying, "Keep your ear tuned to my voice. Come straight to me and you will be all right." That's the voice of the Holy Spirit. Just listen to Him and He will guide you aright. This is one of the joys of good living, to have a divine Companion along life's pathway.

3. *You know that you are engaged in the greatest work in the world.* I saw an investment chart sometime ago which stated that if you had invested $1,000 in a certain life insurance company in 1928, that investment would now be worth $186,000. That was a good investment. A few men believed in Henry Ford when he started out. They invested $500 in his company and they became millionaires. But when you throw your life into God's service, you are making the greatest investment in the world. It is an investment that will pay dividends for time and eternity.

4. *You know that you are living by the best set of rules in the world.* These rules are contained in both the Old Testament and the New Testament. Live by them and you will never go wrong. A man went into a barbershop to get a haircut and the shine boy took his hat. "Don't you want it cleaned, mister?" asked the boy. And the man said, "No, it looks all right." Then the boy did a smart thing. He put the hat on a rack between two brand new hats and it looked pretty disgraceful. The man said to the boy, "I have changed my mind. Take the hat and see that it gets a good cleaning." So we look at our lives and we are satisfied with them. But if we put them alongside God's rules for living, we see our need to live better. We can thank God for the rules that He has given us.

5. *You know that death holds no fear for you.* A man who hasn't moved up to good living in Jesus Christ has a

right to fear death. Death will cut off everything good for him. It will end every chance that he has. Oh, I pity the man who faces death without the Great Friend, Jesus Christ. At best not one of us has many more years to live. Isn't it wonderful to know that all will be well with your soul when that time comes?

A missionary and his family were in China during an air raid. They had no dugout, so the missionary and his wife and their little girl crawled under a table. As the bombs dropped nearby they bowed their heads and prayed. When the danger was over the little girl said, "Daddy, the Lord Jesus is the best Dugout, isn't He?" Oh, when we come to the end of the way, we will come to know as never before that Jesus is the safest refuge for the soul.

6. *You know that you have a home in heaven waiting for you.* John was the apostle of love. He wrote the fourth book in the New Testament. He leaned upon Jesus' breast at the Last Supper. When he was nearly one hundred years old he was banished to the Isle of Patmos. As evening came on I imagine that he climbed to the top of a high hill and looked toward Palestine. His home and his loved ones were there. But he was separated from them by the sea. So God let him look into heaven and told him to write down the words, "And there was no more sea." He knew then that a time was coming when he would never be separated from the people and the things that he loved. Oh, that's our portion, too! Out yonder we will never be separated from God nor our loved ones nor all that is good and glorious and wonderful. That is the climax of good living.

Have you learned the real joy of good living? It comes from trusting Christ, from loving Him and following Him. It is a joy that lasts through all the golden years of eternity. And just remember that good living can bring joy, not only to you, but to others.

A preacher was holding a meeting in a certain place. When he gave the invitation a woman of wealth and distinction came up to confess Christ. She asked permission to say a few words. She was granted this permission and she said, "Maybe you want to know why I came forward. It was not because of the sermon or the song. I came because of the influence of a little woman in this congregation. She has served in my home for many years. I never have known her to do or say an unkind thing. On the other hand, I know many unselfish things that she has done. I often sneered at her religion and laughed at her faithfulness. But when my baby died, she was the one who caused me to look beyond the grave and shed my first tears of hope. The sweetness of her life led me to Christ. I covet the thing that made her life so beautiful."

Oh, may God help us to learn to live in such a way that someone else will say, "I have seen Jesus in your life."

7

From Sinking Sands He Lifted Me

Psalm 40:2

There are many things in our evangelistic churches today, but one thing is sadly lacking. That is the old time testimony meeting. I have been to some of these meetings where a man would stand up and tell what the Lord had done for him and every eye would be upon him and every ear would be listening. If we could get a sincere, genuine, consecrated Christian to come to the pulpit every Sunday night, using a different one each week, to tell of his conversion experience, that would probably have more effect than any sermon the pastor could preach.

In the Psalms we find a man who really loved to give his testimony. Many times David said, "Listen and let me tell you what the Lord has done for me." So here in the fortieth Psalm he says, "I was in a pit, sinking down into the miry clay. But the Lord came and lifted me up. He put my feet on solid rock and put a new song in my mouth." Now let's see the picture here. Yonder is a man deep down in a pit. It is dark down there, but we can see enough to know that he is sinking. He is helpless and hopeless. There is no way to get him out of there; he is going to die. Then we see a stronger man coming. He sees the poor fellow's plight. He reaches down and takes hold of the man. He lifts him up, up, up. Soon he has brought the man out of the pit. He doesn't throw him back into the pit, but he puts him on a rock where he cannot sink. The man is so happy that he begins to sing a song of praise for his rescuer.

We look a little closer and we see that the man in the

67

pit is a lost soul, sinking down into hell. The strong man who pulled him out was the Lord Jesus Christ. Now the man's feet are on the Rock of Ages and he is singing the praise of his Saviour. This man received four things when he came up out of the pit.

I. HEALING

I am not speaking here of physical healing, although I know that God does that. I believe in divine healing but not so much in "divine healers." I have seen cases of sick people where the doctor had given up all hope. Then prayer was offered and healing came. Then the doctor said, "I don't understand it. This healing came from a Higher Source. No earthly skill or medicine could have done it." That is divine healing. It is not a man grabbing someone and shaking him and crying, "Come out of him," but it is God. It is God quietly laying His healing hand upon a sufferer.

But I am speaking here about spiritual healing. All the way through the Bible sin is looked upon as a disease. It is a dread disease which cuts down every man and carries him toward hell. Every one of us is afflicted with this disease. We have "all sinned and come short of the glory of God." "There is not a man upon the earth that doeth good and sinneth not." Since all of us are afflicted with this disease, all of us need healing. And Jesus, going out to Calvary, furnishes that healing for us. When we come to Him, we are healed of our spiritual sickness.

A Chicago salesman was addicted to strong drink. One day he was riding with some of his associates in a pullman car. A flask of whisky was produced, but he said, "No, I am not drinking any more." They laughed at him for they thought that he was joking. But when they saw that he was serious they asked, "Are you sick?" "No," said the man, "but a few weeks ago my business took me into a pawnshop. While I was there a young man came in. He was fully clad and shivering from the cold. He handed the pawnbroker a package and said, 'Give me ten cents for these.' The pawnbroker opened the package and found a pair of baby shoes. He said to the man, 'You are certainly not going to sell these shoes, are you? Your baby needs them more than you need the money for liquor.' And the man replied, 'No, my baby doesn't need these shoes. She died last night. Give me the money quick.'" Then the man on the train said, "When I looked at that poor fellow and realized the hopelessness of his life and the sadness of his home, I saw what I might be in ten or fifteen years. I found a quiet place and cried out, 'Oh, God, help me and save me for Jesus sake!' And He did save me and gave me the victory. I will not be drinking with you any more."

Oh, my friend, this may not be your sin, but without Christ you are going down with a dread disease and only the blood of Christ can save you. Suppose that you were sick and the doctor came and said, "In your present condition you can't live forty-eight hours. But I have some wonderful medicine here. I have had a thousand patients with this same disease. I gave them this medicine and everyone is healthy today. You can lie there and die or you can take the medicine and get well." What would you do? Surely you would grasp the bottle and cry out, "Give me the medicine now." Well, Jesus is the remedy for sin. Millions of those who were sinking down to hell have come to Him. He has never lost a patient. He can heal spiritual sickness. The first thing that Christ gives to anyone who comes to Him is healing.

II. Help

It isn't enough for a baby to be born and left alone. That baby needs help and nourishment and these are provided. It is wonderful to be born again. It is glorious to be saved. But the battle is not over. It has just begun. You are going to need help. And the gracious Saviour says, "I will help you. I will stand by your side. I will never leave thee nor forsake thee."

What would we do if we did not have Christ to help us? You may have had a conversion experience as great as that of Paul, but you are still going to need the Lord's help. What would you do in the hour of sorrow if you could not hear Him say, "Let not your heart be troubled"? What would you do in the time of need if you could not hear the words, "My God shall supply every need of yours"? What would you do when your friends forsake you if you could not hear the words, "When your mother and father forsake you, then I will take you up"? What would you do when you are lonely if you could not hear the words, "The Lord is my Shepherd"? What would you do when things go wrong if you could not hear the words, "All things work together for good to them that love God"?

The title of one of our songs is, "No one ever cared for me like Jesus." Oh, it is true. He does care. And from the moment that you trust Him as Saviour until the day that He takes you to glory, He will look after you and help you. I went to the hospital to see a woman who had undergone a delicate throat operation. I asked her the quetsion, "How did you get along?" She replied, "I knew that this was a very serious operation, so as they rolled my bed out of the room and toward the operating room I closed my eyes and talked to God. I turned everything over to Him. I told Him that I was ready to die and come to Him or ready to live and serve Him. Then peace came to my soul and I was not afraid. He brought me through." Come on, you sinners, you who do not have a Saviour. Where are you going to get any help like that? There is no help for you if you don't know Jesus. This is a tough old world and there are troubles on every side. I wouldn't dare to face them alone. But Jesus offers healing and then He provides help.

III. Hope

An automobile won't run without gasoline, a watch will not run without winding and flowers will not grow without sunshine and water. Neither can a man go on without hope. If a man looks toward tomorrow and has no hope, he might as well be dead. Well, where can a man find hope for tomorrow? Can he find it in his money? No, he can lose that very easily. Can he find hope in his friends? No, they may forsake him. Can he find hope in his good life? No, everyone of us has sinned. The only hope that a man has is in Jesus Christ. What do you have to hold on to if you have never placed your hand in the nail-pierced hand of Christ?

Yonder are two men dying. I go to see them and I say to the first one, "Sir, what is your hope?" And he replies, "Well, I have never been a bad man. It is true that I am not a Christian and I never joined a church. But I never harmed anybody. I try to treat everyone kindly. I have paid my bills and I have given to every good cause. I have been a pretty good fellow, after all." And as I watch him die, I see a man going into eternity with his hands clasping emptiness. He is dying without God and without hope.

Then I say to the other man, "Sir, what is your hope?" And his face lights up and I hear him say, "My hope is built on nothing less than Jesus' blood and righteousness, I dare not trust the sweetest frame, but wholly lean on Jesus' Name." And suddenly the room is filled with sunshine and I feel God's presence there. Then I hear the angels singing as I watch a soul being wafted to his heavenly home.

What would you take for your Christian hope? Surely there is not enough money in the world to buy it. Christ gives healing, then He provides help, then He fills the soul with hope.

IV. HEAVEN

Christ gives a man four things: healing, help, hope, heaven. Yet some men are so foolish as to say, "I don't want Christ. I don't want all these things that He gives." Paul tells us that if we have no hope beyond this world, we are of all men most miserable. If a man suffers pain for many days and the doctor can promise no relief, he indeed becomes a miserable man. A few years ago I had a serious operation. Three-fourths of my stomach was removed. For days and nights the pain was excruciating. I didn't want anything to eat or drink for seven weeks. If I hadn't been able to look forward to something better, I would have been a most miserable man. So if a man lives here for fifty or sixty or seventy years and has nothing waiting for him at the end of the way, he is not living, he is just existing.

But let me tell you that heaven is waiting out there for the Christian. Christ promised to take to heaven all those who put their trust in Him. He never breaks a promise. Maybe you gave your heart to Him when you were ten years of age. You may not die until you are ninety years of age, but God will keep the promise He made eighty years before that time to a little boy. You haven't always been what you should have been. You have committed many sins and you have displeased Him often. But He promised to take you home and He will certainly do that.

Two heathen women went to the cemetery to the graves of their little babies. They wailed, they mourned, they cried out to their false gods, they threw themselves upon the graves, but nothing happened. Then they looked up and saw a funeral procession. A missionary and his wife were laying their little baby away. As they stood by the grave the heathen women could see the peace of God written on their faces. One of the women said, "Why don't they weep and cry out as we do?" And the other one replied, "They have some kind of hope that they will see their baby again." Ah yes, heaven is out yonder waiting for us. It is a glorious place of joy and happiness. It is a place where all sin and sorrow are left out. It is a place where we will see our loved ones again. It is a place where we will see Jesus and be with Him forever.

So here is what Christ offers you today. He offers you healing, which means the forgiveness of all sin. He offers you help along life's pathway. He offers you hope for all the days to come. He offers you heaven at the end of the way. Why don't you open up your heart and receive all that He has to offer you?

Some years ago five men were entombed in a Kentucky mine. Only one was a Christian. During those dark days this Christian man led three of the others to Christ. But one man would not yield. When it seemed that all hope was gone, the Christian soul-winner said to the unsaved man, "Fred, I am going to write a message for our friends to read when they find our bodies. I will tell them that four of us have been saved. What can I tell them about you?" The man hesitated for a minute and then he cried out, "I will give my heart to Christ. Write down that I was saved." These men were later rescued, but there in the depths of the earth four lost men had found Christ as their Saviour.

What do you want written about you? Do you want the record to say, "He rejected Christ and was lost forever"? Or do you want the record to say, "He was saved, saved by the blood of the crucified Christ"?

8

Mr. Chairman, I Nominate This Man

Matthew 27:22

Every four years we have a presidential election in the United States. Several months before the November election date the political parties meet and nominate men for this high office of president of our country. The cities are crowded. The hotels are full. Thousands of delegates attend the sessions of these conventions. Millions of people watch the proceedings on television. A platform is adopted and nominating speeches are made. Out of all this chaos two men become the nominees for the office. In November the people go to the polls and vote for the man of their choice. This is the privilege and the duty of every American citizen.

However, I want to nominate another man for your consideration. I would like to recommend Him to you as the Saviour of your soul and the Lord of your life. You know that I am talking about the Lord Jesus Christ. With all my heart I commend Him to you. I commend Him to you for today, for tomorrow, for life, for death, for eternity. When you listen to the political speeches in a campaign you hear the worst things about the candidates. An Englishman who came to America said, "It is a strange thing, but I believe you Americans are running the two worst men in your country for the presidency." But let me tell you this — no one truthfully could ever say anything against Jesus Christ. His friends and His enemies must join with Pilate in saying, "I find no fault in this just man."

I. Who Is This Man?

1. *He is the eternal Son of God.* He existed with the Father before the world began. "In the beginning was the Word, and the Word was with God, and the Word was God." Go back into the dateless past and you will find Jesus Christ on the bosom of the Father. It is true that He was born more than nineteen hundred years ago in Bethlehem of the Virgin Mary. This was just God's way of getting His Son into the world. The Bible tells us that He "became flesh and dwelt among us." God could have sent Him into the world full-grown, but He wanted Him to grow up as a normal child. He wanted Him to go through all of the trials and temptations that we have so that He could always help us.

It is wonderful to be the child of a king or the son of a president, or the child of a great and good man. But how much more wonderful to be the Son of the Eternal God. No wonder He had power to still the storms and calm the seas. He made them. He was the Son of God with power.

Because He was God's Son there was no sin in Him. Can you imagine a man living in this world over thirty-three years and never having any sinful thought, word or deed? You can't imagine a human being living that way, but Jesus was more than a mere man. He was God's Son. A child cannot walk through water without getting his feet wet. A man cannot handle coal without getting his hands blackened. Neither can he live in a sinful world without becoming stained with sin. But Jesus Christ came into a sinful world, walked through it, touched men full of sin, yet never became tainted with sin. He said on one occasion, "Satan has nothing in Me." He could say that because He was the Son of God. I recommend Him to you.

2. *He is a wonderful servant of mankind.* When you see Him go through the world He walks not as a God, but as a man, as a servant of mankind. He said, "I am among you as One who serves." He proved this statement by

spending every moment in service to others. He goes down the road and meets a blind man. Soon the blind man can see. He meets a deaf man and soon the deaf man can hear. He meets a crippled man and soon that man is walking, leaping and praising God. A poor, dying leper approaches Him and soon that leper is well and whole and strong. A distraught father weeps over a dead child and soon that child is brought back to life. What did Jesus get out of all this? He charged no fees. He thought only of serving others. This was His joy and His reward.

Oh yes, He went home to heaven, but He is still serving mankind. He is always ready to help us. He tells us to call upon Him in the time of our need. No man ever had such a record of wonderful service to this old world.

3. *He is the Saviour of the world.* Ah, that's where He has done His greatest work. He came into the world, not merely to heal or to teach, but to save souls. From the starry heights of heaven He looked down and saw men in sin. They were lost, they were going down to death and hell. So He hurried to earth and to the cross to save them.

Now there would have been no saving power in Him if He had not gone to the cross. He lived a useful life and set a wonderful example for us. But we are not saved by His example. He gave to the world its loftiest principles. He gave us the Golden Rule and other great teachings. But we are not saved by the teachings of Christ. We are saved only because He paid the price of our sins when He shed His blood upon the cross. When you come that way, by the way of the cross, you can find salvation.

In a Southern city a fine man was engaged to a beautiful woman. They had a lover's quarrel and the engagement was broken. A little later the man was seriously ill in the hospital. A doctor friend, who knew of this break with the man's sweetheart, ministered to him. Yet the man failed fast. He had no interest in getting well. Finally the doctor went to the woman and said, "Your friend is mighty sick.

He has passed the critical stage, yet he is dying." "How can that be?" she asked. The doctor replied, "The disease is past the critical stage, but he doesn't want to live. He is dying of an undying love for you." The woman asked the doctor to go with her to the flower shop. She bought a beautiful bouquet and wrote on a card these words, "With all my love." She signed the card and gave the flowers to the doctor to be carried to the man. The man was asleep when the doctor went to his room so he left the room and went to another part of the hospital. When he came back a little later, the man thanked him for the flowers. The doctor said, "The flowers are not from me. Look at the card." The man looked at the card and saw the name and the words, "With all my love." An instant change came over the man. He sent for his sweetheart and they made up their differences. As soon as he was out of the hospital they were married.

We were like that. We were dying with sin. But the One who loved us had the cure. He came down to earth and went to the cross. He gave Himself away for us. On that cross He could have written the words, "With all My love." Yes, He was born to die. He loved us and gave Himself for us. Let me tell you that He is wonderful.

4. *He is our final judge.* Here is a solemn fact that ought to cause every man to stop and think. You can go through life and have a fine time and enjoy many things. But just remember that there is a reckoning time, a payday, a judgment.

Listen to this scripture: "It is appointed unto man once to die and after that the judgment." If the Lord does not come back soon every one of us will go through the experience of death. But that is not all. There is a judgment beyond death. There is no escaping that judgment. Your wealth, your power, your position will not help you to escape. Every man, whether he be rich or poor, great or small, must stand before the judgment bar of God. And this Saviour who loved you, died for you and knows all about you will sit upon the throne as your judge and your jury.

In 1883 one of the islands in the Mediterranean was a famous summer resort for the Italians. The scientists of that day heard certain rumblings underground, indicating that an earthquake was coming. The hotel men would not allow this news to be published for fear that their business would be ruined. The crowds came that summer and in the middle of the season the earthquake came, bringing death to hundreds of people. They refused to heed the warnings. On every side you and I are also being warned of death and the judgment. Heart disease and cancer and accidents are rushing people into eternity. You will do well to heed these warnings, for soon every one of us will come face to face with the judge and the judgment.

II. What Is This Man's Record?

We know who He is, now let us examine His record.

1. *He has saved all who have come unto Him.* That is His promise and the record tells us that He has kept His promise. He said, "Come unto me, all ye that labour and are heavy laden, and I will give you rest." He said, "Look unto me, and be ye saved, all the ends of the earth." He said, "Him that cometh to me I will in no wise cast out." John said, "As many as received him, to them gave he power to become the sons of God." We are not to look to ourselves or our own goodness and righteousness. We are to look to Jesus. He is the only one who can save.

Once upon a time there was a man who hated Christ. He belonged to the opposition party. He did all he could to destroy Christ and His followers. He even put many of them to death. The trouble with him was that he did not know Christ. Then one day he met Him on the Damascus Road. This meeting transformed that man. No longer was Christ his enemy, He was his best Friend. No longer did he speak evil of Christ, he said the best things about Him that have ever been said. The story of this man is given in the Bible. It is the story of how Jesus saves all who come unto Him. He wants everyone to come to Him for salvation. He calls by His Spirit, by a sermon, by a song, in many other ways. He always receives those who come. No matter how sinful nor how far away from God they are, His record shows that He receives all those who come unto Him.

2. *He has never let His people down.* Some people have the idea that after we are saved, if we don't live up to the letter of the law or if we get off the beam, He will permit us to be lost. Oh, we are too weak to live perfect lives. All of us are going to hell if salvation depends upon perfection. Here is a train going to New York City. I buy my ticket and get on the train. It is not up to me to get myself to New York, it is up to the train and the crew. We may not get there, we may have a wreck. But that is not my responsibility, it is theirs. It is just my responsibility to buy the ticket and get on the train.

Well, Jesus promises to take us to glory. Through repentance and faith we meet His conditions. Then it is up to Him to take us home. If I must depend upon my own works to get me to heaven, salvation is not by the grace of God. The whole Bible is against such teaching. Now, whereas the train might not get us to New York, we know that Jesus never fails. He begins a good work in us and completes it unto the day of redemption. One of our deacons is a magician. Sometime ago in performing a certain trick he dropped a glass. He said that he had been performing this trick for thirty years and that was the first time he had dropped the glass. This is a good record, but Jesus has a better one. He has saved millions over the years and never has dropped even one.

3. *He has comforted His people in the time of sorrow.* He certainly has a good record here. He loved Mary and

Martha and Lazarus who lived in the little town of Bethany. Once when He was away on a preaching mission Lazarus died. When He came back the weeping sisters said, "Lord, if you had been here our brother would not have died." He not only comforted them, but He brought their brother back to them. We must remember that Christ will comfort us in our sorrow and that one day He will give our loved ones back to us. We will have them then, not as they went away, but in perfect health.

My phone rings and the news comes to me that one of my members has just died. I go to the home and I find that the friends and neighbors are already there. They are doing all that they can for the weeping widow. They clean the house, they prepare the meals, they speak as sweetly as they can. I go into the home and I take the hand of the bereaved one, I express my sympathy and offer a prayer. That is about all that the neighbors and I can do to comfort the one who is in sorrow. Then I think of how little this is compared to what Jesus does. He puts His arms of grace around us. He speaks peace to our souls. He causes us to know that "all things work together for good to them that love God."

4. *He has answered the prayers of His people.* He has a good record there, too. He promised to answer our prayers and He keeps that promise. Oh, that we might realize the power of prayer! Prayer has power in our personal lives. It will make us better people. The man who really prays doesn't continue in sin. The man who really prays adopts a right attitude in his heart. The man who really prays is faithful to Christ and His church and His service.

Oh, spiritual weaklings that we are, why don't we link ourselves to His power in prayer? Why do we go faltering and stumbling through life when God offers us better things? In times past God's people called on Him in prayer and He heard their cries and answered their prayers. He will do the same for us.

5. *He has met His people at the gates of Glory.* The Christian is not alone in the hour of death. "Precious in the sight of the Lord is the death of his saints." We need not fear death, we need not fear to grapple with this monster. The One who conquered death has promised to be with us.

Sometimes we think of the things that we want to do here. We think about our plans for the future, and we look forward to many responsibilities and many joys. Then we think about death and our selfish side says, "I want to live and enjoy these things." Then a still small voice whispers and says, "Out beyond death there is a life a million times more wonderful than this. Let your heart look up and look forward toward those things." It is still true that "to live is Christ and to die is gain." So when we come to the river at the closing of day we will not have to cross Jordan alone. Jesus will be waiting to escort us to our heavenly mansion.

So come and examine the record of Christ. It is a perfect record in every way. It is especially wonderful in relation to His children.

III. What Does This Man Promise?

1. *He promises to adopt us into His family.* I am thinking now of a dear little girl who was born to a sinful woman and a thoughtless man. She didn't have a chance. They didn't want her. They were willing to abandon her and let her die. Then a fine Christian couple moved in and adopted the child. They showered her with love and gave her the best they had. We are like that little child. We were lost without hope and without God. Then Christ came in and adopted us into His family. He wrote our name in His book. He gave us a home in heaven. Now we are His and His forever. Yes, He promises to adopt all those who come to Him by faith.

2. *He promises to be with us always.* When we hear that sweet promise we realize that we never have to walk

alone. All along our pilgrim journey we can lean on the Everlasting Arms. But always remember this — we can't expect Him to walk with us unless we are walking His way. That way is the way of righteousness and faithfulness and service and love.

A woman called an Atlanta preacher and said, "I want you to go and see a friend of mine. She heard you preach once and said that she enjoyed it. Maybe you can help her." So the preacher and his wife went to this lovely home. They were graciously received and had a delightful visit. As they left the home the preacher said to his wife, "There is something wrong here. I wonder why I was sent to this home. It's a lovely home and they seem to be spendid people." The next morning the preacher's phone rang and the woman whom he had visited said, "I wondered why you came to see us yesterday, but now I know. I had planned to commit suicide. I hid the poison just before you came in. After you had gone I told myself that maybe God cared after all. I would like to talk to you. May I come to your study?" The woman came to the church and told the preacher a sordid story. She and her husband had been active in a church in Texas before they moved to Atlanta. He became very busy and had little time for her and no time for the church. She joined a club where everybody signed a pledge that they would not go to any of the meetings with their own husband or wife, but with someone else's. She started going to these meetings and now she confessed that she had been untrue to her husband and didn't want to live any longer. The preacher said, "You have a wonderful background. How did all of this happen? What was the cause of it?" The woman answered, "I believe that there is one major cause for my trouble and I wish that I could tell every trunk Baptist in the world about it. I attribute my trouble to the fact that we were so foolish as to try to live our lives in a great city without a church home and without God."

Oh, yes, sin and sorrow come when you leave Him out. So let me advise you not to try to live out of the church and away from God. He promises to be with you always as long as you walk in His way and His will.

3. *He promises to take us home to heaven.* Heaven is not just an imaginary place, like Utopia or Shangri-la. It is just as real as the city in which you live. Jesus has gone to prepare that place for us. It is ready now. At the end of the way He will take us home. But remember that heaven is a prepared place for a prepared people. The only ones who are prepared are those who have come to Christ.

A man dreamed that he was constructing a ladder from earth to heaven. Every time he did a good deed a rung was added to the ladder. Every time he gave some money to a good cause another rung was added. He felt sure that because of his good deeds the ladder would soon reach to heaven. He climbed to the top of the ladder and felt sure that he was just a step from heaven. Then he heard a voice saying, "I am the way. He that climbeth up some other way is a thief and a robber." Then the ladder came crashing down. He woke up and realized his mistake. He came to the foot of the cross, turned away from all of his sin, trusted Christ and was saved. Yes, He promises to take us home to heaven if we come to Him and we can bank on that promise.

I have told you who Jesus is. I have given you His record. I have told you about His platform of promises. Now what are you going to do with Him? Lost man, what are you going to do with Him? The rich young ruler stood where you stand. He had to make a choice. On one side there was the world and all of its riches. On the other side there was Christ and heaven. He made the wrong choice. He chose the world and went away from Christ. And we read that He went away in sorrow. You, too, will go away in sorrow if you reject Christ. Life will never be what it ought to be and at the end of the way there is nothing awaiting you but doom.

Christian, what are you going to do with Jesus? He has saved you. Are you going to give Him first place in your heart and life or just the tiny corners of your heart and life? A man who was a prosperous business man was converted and called to preach. He turned his back upon his business and gave up everything for the ministry. His wife, who was a society leader, objected strenuously to his decision. She said, "I didn't marry a preacher. I married a business man, hoping that we would have plenty of money to live on." Although she rebelled the man went on with his preaching. Sometimes on Sunday morning when he would start out to preach in his country church, she would go out and lie down across the driveway in an effort to prevent his leaving. But he kept on faithfully for the Lord. In the providence of God she was converted. She became a devout Christian and a great help in her husband's ministry.

God help us to find His will for our lives. Like this preacher we should let nothing keep us from giving Him our best. So will our lives be happy and useful here and so will eternal joys be ours at the end of the way.

9

Salvation of the Whole Man

I Thessalonians 1:1-10

The Lord Jesus Christ died on a Roman cross between two thieves. One of these thieves certainly must have been touched by the Spirit of God, for he looked up to Christ in faith and cried out, "Lord, remember me when thou comest into thy kingdom." And Jesus answered, "This day shalt thou be with me in paradise." So Christ took this man home to heaven and he has been there ever since. I am sure that since that time many other men have been saved in the last moments of life. But that is the salvation of the soul only. It is not salvation of the whole man.

Salvation of the whole man includes salvation of life as well as salvation of soul. That is the reason that we plead with people to give themselves to Christ early in life. In my text Paul is writing of the three stages in complete salvation. He explains what had happened to the Thessalonians:

I. They turned to God from idols
II. They served the living and true God
III. They waited for God's Son from heaven

I. THEY TURNED TO GOD FROM IDOLS

That is the beginning of salvation. Everyone who wants to be saved must make a turn. They must turn from self and sin to the Saviour. These people had turned from idols unto God. Now of course none of you has ever worshiped the kind of idols that they worshiped. But an idol is anything chosen above God. You can never be saved until

85

you have turned that thing down and chosen God instead.

Are we making salvation too easy today? The old theologians demanded complete crucifixion of will as a ground for salvation. Paul said, "I am crucified with Christ." Now that meant something. But today we make it too easy. We don't demand much in order for a person to become a member of the church. Then we let them continue as members with even fewer demands upon them. Today a person can do most anything and live most any way and still be in good standing in a church. But getting back to the original point, let me say that turning to God from idols is the beginning of salvation. If some idol is in your heart today, if there is something that takes precedence over the Lord, why not turn from that thing today and come to God through faith in Jesus Christ. A "turning from" is the first point in salvation.

II. The Central Point in Salvation Is Serving God

Our works do not save us, but if we are truly saved we will serve the Lord. "By their fruits ye shall know them." Service to God is one of the fruits of salvation. Now how can we serve Him best?

1. *We can serve God by consecrated Christian living.* The best service you can render God is to lead a consecrated Christian life. No one can fully estimate the power and influence of a good life. The Christians of the first century lived wonderfully for Christ. Their neighbors watched them and soon they were saying, "These people are different. They have been with Jesus." Oh, if we can live in such a way that others can see Jesus in us we will be serving God in a wonderful way.

A young American teacher was employed in a Japanese government school. They gave him to understand that he was never to mention Christ or Christianity to the students. He kept his promise but his life was so pure and his spirit was so kind that the students began to seek for the secret of his life. After a few months a large group of students gave their hearts to the Christ whom they knew he followed. Later some of them entered the ministry. Some people are not able to witness and talk loudly for Christ, but in living good lives they become wonderful witnesses and servants for God.

A Christian man sat at his desk one day, thinking of life in terms of surrender to Christ. It seemed that he could feel the presence of the Master and hear His gentle voice asking for the keys to every room in his heart. So one after another he gladly yielded the keys until only one small key was left. He didn't want to surrender this key. He said, "Master, I can't give up this one. Let me keep just this one from Thee." Then it seemed that the Lord turned sorrowfully away from him. But the young man would not let Him go. He called out, "Master, I haven't the strength to give up this key, please come and take it." Then the Lord turned back and took the key, unlocked that room and possessed it. From that day on the Christian knew a joy and a power that comes only from a wholly surrendered life.

Do you want to serve God in a real way? Then don't hold anything back. Give Him all of the keys. Give up that little sin. Give up that bad habit which keeps you from being a consecrated Christian. Give yourself to Him in complete surrender.

2. *We can serve God by giving Him our time.* Time is a great problem to many people today. You try to get them to do things for God and they say, "I don't have time." Well, everyone has some time which they don't spend in eating and sleeping and working. In fact, the working hours for most people are shorter than ever before. Then why don't they have time to give to the things of Christ? There is just one answer. They are giving too much time to the things of the world, the things that don't count for God,

the things that will die with the setting sun, the things that bring no heavenly reward.

A young woman was the teacher of a Sunday school class. Most of the girls in the class were from poor homes. She had a tremendous opportunity to give out some of her Christian experience and love to these little starved hearts and minds. But one day the superintendent received her resignation. She said that she didn't have time and strength to give to the class. The trouble was that she was mixed up with so many others things. When she became pressed for time the first thing she gave up was her opportunity to serve God. I have seen this same thing happen hundreds of times. Too many Christians are too busy for service to God. They are giving their time and their energy to the institutions and organizations of this world. Is that a sin? Yes, it is a sin to give to the world the time and energy that belongs to God.

I am glad that God is not too busy to serve us. When we were lost He had time to feel sorry for us and give His Son to die for our sins. Today when we need things He has time to provide them. "My God shall supply every need of yours, according to his riches in glory by Christ Jesus." When we need comfort He has time to put His arms around us and say, "Come unto me, all ye that labour and are heavy laden, and I will give you rest." And when we come to the end of the way He will have time to take us to heaven and give us an eternal home. Why can't we treat God a little more like He treats us? Why don't you as a Christian turn away from some of these other things and serve God with your time?

3. *We can serve God by giving Him our talents.* God gives us every talent that we have, and every talent ought to be used for Him. But many people are using their talents for the world instead of God. Other people say that they have no talents, so they do nothing for the Lord. But every one can do something for the Christ who gave His all for

them. If you cannot speak or sing you can at least be faithful and thus be an inspiration to others. Maybe all that you can do is just come to church and give God a tenth of your income. That also is serving God.

A rich woman gave liberally to her church and to missions. But she was not satisfied. She felt that this was not enough, she wanted to do something else. So she went to the mission office and offered her services. They told her that they needed no help except for someone to wrap bundles of literature. She promptly said that she would be glad to do this. So day after day this rich woman came and wrapped the bundles. This was a humble, tedious service, but she gladly gave herself to it. That is what we need today — people who are willing to do anything that they can for God.

A young woman had an unusual talent for playing the violin. She often played at dances but she felt a little uncomfortable in these surroundings. Then one evening she attended a revival service. In that service she heard the Saviour calling her and she gave her heart to Him. But she was not fully satisfied simply by receiving the salvation of her soul. The next evening she came to church again. When the invitation was given at the close of the service she walked down the aisle, carrying her violin. She laid this violin upon the altar. She was simply saying that she wanted both her life and her talent to be consecrated and dedicated to the service of Christ. After that meeting her violin was used only in a way that God could bless it.

Your talents may be small, but if you turn them over to Christ He can use them and you will be happier because of it.

4. *We can serve God by telling others about Christ.* The greatest trust that God has put in our hands is the gospel message of salvation. The old, old story is the one that transforms lives. What would your life be worth today if you had not heard it? What hope would you have if you

didn't know Jesus? Who will tell others about Him if we don't do it? We can tell the story at home in person and we can tell the story around the world through out gifts and our prayers.

A young girl who had just finished college was wondering what her life work would be. She felt that she had no special talents. Then one day she found Jesus Christ as her Saviour. She prayed earnestly, "Lord, if there is anything I can do for Thee, if there is any service that I can render, I am ready." She began to dream about working in some foreign field. But the door to such service seemed closed at the time so she just waited. While she waited she taught a class of junior girls and put her best into the teaching of the Bible and winning the girls to Christ. Years have gone by and she is still teaching in the Junior Department. Every year through her influence the new girls in her class are saved and they join the church. Her life is counting for God right at home. So can yours and mine.

Two girls came home from college for the Christmas holidays. The first girl began to plan social events for the holidays — dances, skating parties and other forms of entertainment. Three weeks rushed by and then she went back to college. She had been to church only one time and she was late on that occasion. She never thought of contributing anything to the life of her church during the holidays. The other girl reached home and planned her schedule. She didn't forget Christ. One afternoon she invited to her home some of the girls who had not been invited to any parties. Among them there was one girl who was not a Christian. They had a wonderful time. The Christian girl did not hesitate to tell what Christ meant to her life. She went back to college in a happy frame of mind. Two weeks later she received a letter from the lost girl telling that she had been saved, had joined the church and was trying to serve the Lord. Even a vacation can be used for the glory of God. You can serve God by telling others about His Son.

5. *We can serve God by the right use of our money.*
The least that any Christian ought to give is the tithe. This
ought to be given to God through the local church. This
vein of teaching runs all through the Bible. Every Christian
owes God at least a tenth of his income, then the other
nine-tenths is to be used rightly for His glory. And when
you give God His tenth the other nine-tenths goes farther.
Every Christian can testify to this fact.

In a recent article a preacher said that if a Christian
tried tithing for one year, he couldn't give it up. He simply
meant that God would bless that Christian in such a manner that he couldn't afford to give up tithing. Oh, I hear
someone saying, "I tried to tithe and I had a harder time
than ever." You mean that you started tithing and then
when something happened you quit tithing. You didn't
give God a chance. If you live a consistent Christian life
and give God His part, I know that He will bless you. He
promises to do so and He always keeps His promise.

Did you ever think of what the church has done for
you? It cared for you in the nursery as a baby. It provided
a Sunday school where you were taught the Bible. Then
it brought the message of salvation to you and helped you
to find Christ. The church prays for you when you are
sick, brings you comfort in time of sorrow and welcomes
you back when you have gone astray. Every other institution asks who you are and what you have to offer. The
church opens wide its arms and says, "No matter who you
are, come in and let us help you." Christ put the church
here to help you. It will help you if you give it a chance.
Don't you think you owe the church something? Don't you
think you owe God something? God says that you owe
Him at least a tenth and this tenth is to go through the
church.

In Texas some years ago there was a preacher who
was making $1,500 per year. He believed in tithing but
he had a big family and felt that he couldn't take care of

his family if he tithed. He simply didn't have enough faith. Then a rich man who did tithe offered him a challenge. He said, "I want you to tithe every month. If you ever miss the money or need it just write to me and I will send you a check to cover what you have given." The agreement was made and the preacher began giving a tithe every month. Things worked out so well and God blessed him so richly that he never had to ask the wealthy man for a cent. At the end of the year he was very happy that he had been tithing. But then he was filled with shame. He had believed the rich man who had told him that he would stand by him if he tithed, but he hadn't believed the God who had offered to do the same thing. Outside of your salvation one of the biggest blessings that can come to you is learning to trust God. He said that He would take care of you if you brought His tithe into the storehouse. Don't you believe it?

Now God doesn't need our financial help. He owns everything. Tithing is not just a case of God trying to get our money. He knows what tithing will mean to us. Therefore He graciously gives every Christian an opportunity to co-operate with Him. He wants us to love Him, to trust Him and put Him first. Then the Almighty God of heaven promises to take care of us.

The secretary of the British Mission Society called upon a merchant to help financially in some special mission work. The merchant wrote out a check for $250.00. Just then a cablegram was handed him. He said to the mission secretary, "One of my ships has been lost at sea. This makes a great difference in my affairs, I will have to change the check." The secretary said that he understood and handed the first check back to the merchant. The merchant then gave him another check and to his surprise he learned that it was written for $1,000.00. He told the man that he must have made a mistake. Then the merchant said, "No, I haven't made a mistake. I read between the lines of this cablegram and I saw the words, 'Lay not up for yourselves treasures upon the earth.'"

Christ gave the great commission to His church. He has told us to go into all the world with the Gospel message. The only way you can do this is through the budget of your church. The work of that budget starts at home and extends to the ends of the earth. Don't be a little, narrow, selfish Christian. Get into the entire program of your church and let the stream of your money and influence go out to the ends of the earth.

A lighthouse stood on a rugged coast and many ships and many lives were in the keeping of the man who ran the lighthouse. Each month he received just enough fuel to last one month. But one day a woman came and asked for some oil for her stove so that she could warm her only child. The man gave her this oil. Then he gave some oil to a father so that his son might read at night. Then he gave another man some oil that was needed for his engine. He kept on giving out this fuel and near the end of the month his supply was gone. That night the light in the lighthouse went out. There was a storm on the sea the same night. A ship went down and scores of people lost their lives. The next morning a government agent came to the lighthouse and said to the keeper, "Last night your light was out and a ship went down." The keeper began telling him how he had given the fuel out for good causes. Then the agent said to him, "You were given one task above all others. You were to keep this light burning. The other demands for fuel were secondary. Your light went out, the ship went down and scores were lost. For this there is no defense."

My friend, we are the lighthouse-keepers of the world. We have one task above all others. We are to keep the Gospel lights burning. We have no right to take the oil for God's light and use it on something else. It is all right for you to pay for your home. It is all right for you to ride in a nice car and have many of the comforts of life. But you must not take away from God's money. The Bible teaches that the "tithe is the Lord's." You have no more right to take that money and use it for yourself than you have the right to rob a drug store cash register and use that money for yourself.

The wonder and the beauty of giving is the way that God pays off. A man who lives faithfully for Christ and tithes his income is paid off in this world and the world to come. God will take care of you down here. He will fill your life with blessings, both material and spiritual. At the end of the way He will have a reward in heaven for you. You can't outgive God — you can't improve on God's way. I challenge you to tithe and watch Him bless you.

III. They Waited for His Son From Heaven

I do not have time to dwell on this thought. We are to turn from idols, we are to serve the living God, and we are to wait for His Son from heaven.

Yes, one day we are going to face Christ. When we meet Him face to face surely we want to be able to say, "Lord, I did my best for You." Then He will smile and say, "Come on in, I am pleased with what you have done." And when we see that smile we will know that it was worth it all to follow Him and give Him our best.

10

Weighed in the Balances and Found Wanting
(Part One)

Daniel 5:27

Today we journey back to ancient Babylon and look in upon a royal banquet. This banquet was given by Belshazzar, the young and haughty king. The palace was a blaze of light. The long tables were set up for a thousand guests. The light from many candelabras shone upon the gold and silver dishes. The most prominent people in the country were there. They reclined at the tables. They were clad in rich garments, their fingers and arms were ringed with priceless jewels. The air was heavy with perfume and tremulous with music. The half-clad dancers were weaving in and out among the tables, as they performed the suggestive Asiatic dances. Laughter and jokes were flying back and forth.

The kings and the guests were getting drunker and bolder every hour. The king rejoiced that he had been able to provide his guests with such a good time. As the hours passed, however, the party became a little dull and the king decided to do a daring thing. He called one of the stewards to him, whispered a command in his ear and the steward left the room. The guests wondered what would happen next. Their curiosity was soon gratified. The steward returned, bringing with him the cups of gold and silver which his grandfather had carried away from the temple of Jehovah when he had sacked the city of Jerusalem. "Fill 'em up," cried Belshazzar, "and drink to your king." So they filled the cups of the Lord and drank to the king and to their false gods. The hilarity became more boisterous. Everyone was shouting and drinking and laughing. We can almost hear them cry out, "Who is this God of the Jews? Where is He now? We are the master-race. Have another drink from the sacred cups of the temple. Ha, ha, ha, ha!"

Then suddenly a hush like death fell upon the banquet hall. One bleary-eyed fellow shouted, "Look yonder, look at that hand on the wall." And everyone looked and everyone saw the hand. It was a hand without an arm or a body and it was writing in large letters upon the wall. Then the king turned and looked. Immediately he became pale, he began to shake and his knees began to smite against each other. He wondered what all of this meant. Nothing like this ever happened before. So he sent for his wise men, his soothsayers. They came marching in, ready to gain new favor with their king. But when they saw the handwriting on the wall their confidence faded. They couldn't give the meaning. Belshazzar was more shaken up than ever. He didn't know what to do next. Then the queen mother came in. She had heard the confusion. She said to the king, "Don't worry, there is one man in the kingdom wiser than all others. His name is Daniel. He can interpret this writing and give you the meaning of it."

So the king sent for Daniel. When Daniel came in the king began to flatter him. He said, "I have heard that you are a great and wise man. If you will tell me what this writing means I will give you many rich presents and make you third ruler of the kingdom." Then God's man replied, "I don't want any of your gifts. Give them to another. But I will tell you what the writing means. First, I must tell you why it came. You know how your grandfather was blessed of God, then you know how he turned away from the Lord and finally how he humbled himself and came back to God. But you lifted yourself up against God. You haven't glorified Him. You had the audacity to take the vessels out of God's house and use them to drink wine from, while you praised the gods of wood and stone. This is the reason why these things were written on the wall."

"Now," continued Daniel, "here is what the writing means. God says that you are through, your time is up, you are finished. You have been weighed in the balances and found wanting. Now your kingdom will be divided and given to the Medes and Persians."

This was sad new for Belshazzar, but he kept his promise and set Daniel up as a third ruler in the kingdom. All this time the army of Cyrus was just outside the city walls. Now the River Euphrates ran under the wall. So Cyrus had his soldiers dig a channel and turn the river into another direction, then he and his army marched dry-shod into the city. And that night Belshazzar the king was slain. As you see his body lying dead there in the banquet hall you come to realize anew that you can't trifle with God.

In these two messages let us think of the words which were written on the wall. They mean, "Thou art weighed in the balances and found wanting." Belshazzar was not weighed in the balance of public opinion. The people would have said, "He is a great statesman. He is one of our finest young men." He was not weighed in the balances of his own estimation of himself, for he thought himself to be a mighty fine fellow. He was weighed in the balances of God. God examined him and said, "In My sight you are altogether rotten. You lack everything good."

There are some people who rank high in popular favor. They are big folk in the eyes of the world, their names and pictures are often seen in the papers. But they don't weigh an ounce with God. Why is this so? Because they have never seen their need of Him. They have never turned from sin to the Saviour. They are giving their lives away to the things which do not count. Christ is the forgotten man so far as they are concerned.

Now God's balances are found in Exodus 20. We call them the Ten Commandments. How does your life measure up as you compare it with these eternal laws? In these two sermons let us look at these balances.

I. "Thou Shalt Have No Other Gods Before Me"

What is a man's god? It is the thing that he thinks the most of. Some people worship money, it is their god. They will do anything and cut any corner to get it. Some men break into houses to get money, some steal cash from the drawer of the firm where they work. Some have even murdered other people to get their insurance money. Then there are some who will not stoop to these things, but they will put over a shady deal. They will tell a lie about property that they have for sale. They tell this lie to gain more money. Money is their god.

Two young men were working in the basement of a Chicago store. One was a Christian attending the Moody Bible Institute. He was in training to serve Christ. The other young man was not a Christian. The Christian said to him, "Wouldn't you like to be a Christian?" The other man pulled out a roll of bills from his pocket and put them up on the shelf and bowed down in mock worship of them. Then he said, "That's all the Jesus Christ that I want." An hour later these two men were in an elevator accident and both of them were crushed to death. One man went out to meet God after witnessing for Christ, the other went out to meet Him after worshiping money and blaspheming His name.

Some people make social position and prominence their god. They had rather have their name in the newspaper than in the Lamb's Book of Life. They join every club and run after every office. They are hungry for social recognition. I am not saying that every social organization is rotten and wrong, but I am saying that you ought not to put these things before your church and your God. If a choice is to be made, God and His church should come first. Let me say another thing. If you give your best service to God and the church, you will not have time for these other things. After all, why should Christians spend their lives tooting on a tin whistle when they could be playing a pipe organ? At the end of the way, God will not pay off for this worldly service, but He will pay handsomely for the service rendered to the Lord Jesus Christ.

Some people, the Bible says, make appetite their god. We know that it is true. This is why liquor has America in such a deadly grip. Many a man is sacrificing his brain power, his business career, his health, the respect of good people and the love of wife and children because of drink. The Bible over and over speaks out about the evils of strong drink. You can see these effects on every side. Yet some men make appetite their god.

Some people worship the god of pleasure. It is all right to have a good time, but we are not to be a slave to worldly pleasure. A young woman talked to me about dancing and said, "That is my very life." Where are the great crowds on Sunday night? They are not in the churches, they are seeking pleasure and amusement. Many church people even put their television sets ahead of God and His church.

Jesus said that this first commandment was the greatest. He put it in a new way when He said that we are to love God with all of our heart and mind and soul and strength. Some years ago I attended a cowboy camp meeting in the Southwest. That afternoon the men sat around the prayer tree and gave their testimony. One man said, "I ain't no Christian, but I live by the Ten Commandments, so I guess I am all right." I had to tell him that no man except Jesus ever kept the Ten Commandments perfectly. I told him that he was not even keeping the first commandment, for this commandment implies that we are to love God and put Him first. He gave His Son to die for us, and if we put Him first surely we won't reject Him, but we will accept Him as our Saviour. The Ten Commandments do set the standard and we are to try to live up to them. We cannot do this perfectly, but we must depend upon the blood of Christ to make up for our failures.

II. "Thou Shalt Not Make Any Images of God and Worship Them"

It is not wrong to have a picture of Christ on the wall or even to have a small statue of Him. The sin comes in bowing before these objects and worshiping them. How do some people get by with such worship in view of this commandment?

III. "Thou Shalt Not Take the Name of the Lord Thy God in Vain"

I am afraid that many people take this commandment too lightly. Just let some provocation arise and they fill the air with their devil-pleasing, God-defying profanity. One man will say, "I live a good life, I don't drink, I don't steal, I don't commit adultery. But I do swear occasionally." This man thinks he has done nothing wrong. God thinks differently. Oh, this is such a common sin today. If a man wants to write a book that is a best seller, all he has to do is to fill it with profanity and lewd and vulgar language.

A Christian ought to be clean in his speech. If a man knows that you profess to be a Christian and a church member, and if he then hears you cursing, he will have no confidence in your religion. One man said, "When I was saved, I lost half of my vocabulary." That was a good loss. Get your lips out of the gutter and learn to use clean speech at all times. It is easy to judge men by their speech. Sometime ago I was in a downtown store and a man came in who is recognized as a big man in the city. But he couldn't speak one sentence without using a few ugly curse words. When a man talks like that I know that the foundations of his character are rotten. Reverence for God is the foundation of a sound character. When that is gone, character is gone. A man goes down pretty low when he speaks dis-

respectfully of his mother. He goes even lower than that
when he is profane toward God.

You can take the name of the Lord in vain in another
way. You can get on your knees in prayer and not have
a thought of God in your heart. You can recite a ritual
over and over while your mind is a thousand miles away.
I believe that is taking the Lord's name in vain.

Your conversation gives you away, it tells what you
are. Sam Jones said, "When I hear a man cursing and
taking the Lord's name in vain, I hold on to my pocketbook.
I know if he will break one of God's laws, he may break
another." You may not go as far as that, but you must ad-
mit that men show what they are by their speech. Jesus
said, "Out of the abundance of the heart the mouth speak-
eth." Let Jesus fill your heart and the right things will
come out of your mouth.

IV. "Remember the Sabbath Day to Keep It Holy"

People often ask the question, "Why do we observe
the first day of the week instead of the seventh day as they
did in the Old Testament times?" Well, God created the
world. He finished His work in six days and rested on the
seventh. He was commemorating a finished creation. But
now we live in a new dispensation. We don't observe the
Sabbath Day, but the Lord's Day. That is what the New
Testament calls it. On the first day of the week Jesus rose
from the dead. From that day forward the church met on
the first day of the week to commemorate something more
important than a finished creation. They were commemorating a finished redemption.

On Sunday we remember that Jesus rose from the
dead. You get up on Sunday and you put on your best
clothes. You get ready for Sunday school, you take your
Bible in your hand and you start out toward the church.
What are you doing? You are remembering that you are
going to worship One who loved you and died for you and

rose again on the first day of the week. I believe that the whole day belongs to Him. A young man said to me, "If I come to church on Sunday morning and Sunday night, don't you think it would be all right for me to play golf on Sunday afternoon?" And I said to him, "No, the whole day belongs to Him." The services on Sunday morning belong to Him, the services on Sunday evening belong to Him. All the time in between belongs to Him.

Some Christians would never think of playing baseball or picking cotton or buying groceries on Sunday, yet they desecrate the Lord's day in another way. They stay out late Saturday night and then lie in bed until eleven and twelve o'clock on Sunday morning, then lounge around the house all day. They do this instead of going to the Lord's house of worship. That is breaking this commandment.

Many ancient nations came toppling down into oblivion because they violated this command. In many European nations religion has deteriorated and morals have declined because they have violated this command. Is America headed for the rocks because of this same sin, a sin which shows that God has been forgotten? I call on you to treat God's day in the right way. Use it for worship, for rest and for the service of the Lord.

This is as far as I can go in this sermon but I will take up the other commandments in the next message.

I would like to ask you how you stand with God. If God's laws are on one side of the scale and you alone are on the other side, you are going to be found wanting. You will go down forever. But if Jesus is on your side with you, you are safe forevermore.

Sometime ago Dr. Torrey Johnson was on a plane between Chicago and Tulsa. He asked God to give him a chance to talk to someone about Christ. The flight was a bit rough and the stewardess came and sat in the vacant seat beside him. He talked to her and she trusted Christ as her Saviour. Dr. Johnson left the plane at Tulsa. As he said good-by to the stewardess, she pointed toward heaven and said, "If I don't see you down here again, I will see you up there." The next day he read in the newspaper that this same plane had crashed during a storm after it had left Tulsa. The stewardess whom he had won to Christ had been killed. What if she hadn't taken this last chance to take Jesus Christ as her Saviour?

I plead with you to take Him as your Saviour. He will balance the scales for you.

11

Weighed in the Balances and Found Wanting
(Part Two)

Daniel 5:27

In my previous sermon I described a banquet given by Belshazzar, the king of Babylon. In the midst of all the drunken revelry at this banquet, suddenly a hand appeared, writing on the wall. Since the king's soothsayers could not interpret the writing, they called in Daniel, the man of God. He said that the writing meant three things. First, God had finished with this kingdom. It was all over with Belshazzar. Second, he was weighed in the balances and found wanting. Third, the kingdom would be divided and given to the Medes and Persians. And that night Belshazzar was slain and the Medes took over the kingdom.

Now I said that the Ten Commandments were God's balances. They are God's scales with which He weighs men. In the previous sermon I spoke of the first four commandments, in this message I will briefly touch on the last six. We note that the first four commandments have to do with our relationship to God and the last six have to do with our relationship to men. Let us now look at these commandments which concern our relationship to others.

V. "HONOUR THY FATHER AND THY MOTHER, THAT THY DAYS MAY BE LONG IN THE LAND WHICH THE LORD THY GOD GIVETH THEE"

Today we greatly need more honor and more respect for our fathers and mothers. Of course, our fathers and mothers ought to live in such a way that the children can

104

have respect for them. How can a child respect the father
or mother who curses around the house, who comes in with
liquor upon his breath, who has no time to love and counsel
his children. Even so, the children have no right to refer
to their parents as "the old man" or "the old woman."

The Bible says, "Children, obey your parents." This
is one way to honor them. The parents must teach obedience, even if it means many trips to the switch or the
strap. My father shaved with an old-fashioned razor. The
razor strap hung on the back porch and he knew how to
use it, not simply to sharpen the razor, but to sting me
like a thousand bees. Believe me, I knew better than to
disobey him. My mother died when I was four years of
age. My stepmother was a big, strong woman. Believe me,
I remember how strong she was. I remember how she could
use the paddle or the switch. It hurt then and I didn't enjoy
it. But today I thank God for them. They taught me dis-
cipline and obedience and hard work.

Today I hear parents say, "Johnny, don't do that." But
Johnny goes right ahead and does it just the same. Then
they say, "Now, darling, you ought not to do that." But
Johnny pays no attention to that. He becomes disobedient
to his parents, then later in life he disobeys other authorities
and lands in trouble. Some parents say, "I love the little
thing so much that I can't punish him. When he stamps his
foot it is so cute." No, God says that if we love them we
will chasten them for their own good.

Children ought to show more appreciation for their
parents. Some parents slaved to get through school, but
now they fix things up so their children can go through on
a paved highway. The children never stop to think that
they are having it easy because Daddy and Mother made
sacrifices for them. One day you will lose your parents.
Then you will follow them to the grave and say, "I wish I
had been a little more thoughtful. I wish I had been a little

more appreciative." It will be too late then. Now is the time to show your love and appreciation. Now is the time to honor your father and your mother.

VI. "Thou Shalt Not Kill"

"Oh," you say, "preacher, you are not speaking to a group of murderers on death row. We wouldn't think of killing anyone." This is true, but there are other ways of killing people. A husband can kill his wife through cruelty and neglect. A wife can kill her husband through constant nagging. A son or daughter can kill their mother or father through sin. A preacher tells about staying for a week in a lovely home where he was holding a meeting. In the home there was everything that money could buy. He thought that surely the mother of that home must have been perfectly happy. But in the middle of the night she would get up and walk the halls with a breaking heart. She had an only son and he was out living in sin. He was killing her. In a few weeks she died, not of a dread disease, but of a broken heart.

You can be a murderer in your thoughts. The Bible says, "Whosoever hateth his brother is a murderer." This simply means that if you hate anyone you have the seeds of murder in your heart. Do you hate someone so much that you wish they were dead? Then you are violating this commandment in your heart. You wouldn't shoot them to death, because you are afraid of what the law or God would do to you. Yet you wish them dead and that is a sin.

Christians ought to be the kindest people in the world. Of course, they ought not to kill anyone's body, but they ought to be so kind that they will not kill their happiness or peace of mind by anything that they do or say.

VII. "Thou Shalt Not Commit Adultery"

The curse of God always follows the man or woman who breaks this commandment. God shows how He has set His stamp of disapproval upon this sin by showing us in the Bible and in life the terrible consequences which follow.

Look at David. He is one of our heroes, he is one of God's favorites. God called him "a man after my own heart." Then one day David the king, David the mighty man of God, David the hero, David the man after God's own heart, became enamored by a beautiful woman and entered into sin with her. This sin led to another sin, the indirect murder of the woman's husband and finally David's marriage to her. Then several things happened to David. First, he lost his fellowship with God. The man who could write "The Lord is my Shepherd" felt far removed from God. Then trouble began in the family. One tragedy after another came. After a while when his favorite son had been killed, we hear him sobbing, "Oh, Absalom, my son, my son, would God I had died in thy stead." He knew then that his sin was paying off.

Oh, young men and women, be careful. Young people, be careful. Don't trade your future happiness for a few minutes of sinful pleasure. There is too much at stake. Ask God to give you self-control and keep yourself clean for the one that someday you will marry.

VIII. "Thou Shalt Not Steal"

We know that stealing means taking something from another without giving the equivalent in property or money. There are different ways to steal. You steal when you make a false statement about some goods you are selling. You steal when you do like a certain automobile dealer did. I traded automobiles when my car showed on the speedometer that it had been running for 48,000 miles. He turned the speedometer back to 32,000 miles in order to get a better price for the car. You steal when you employ a man and don't give him a good day's pay. You steal when you work for a man and don't give him an honest day's work.

You steal when you gossip about someone and try to rob them of their good name. You steal when you don't pay your honest debts. The Christian, above all people, should pay his debts. He brings a reproach upon the cause of Christ when he doesn't do it.

A certain Christian lived a few miles outside of one of our southern cities. He took the same bus to work every morning. Since it was a thirty minute ride to town he used that time to read his Bible. Of course, the bus driver noticed it. One morning when the man boarded the bus the driver intentionally gave him ten cents too much change. The man walked up the aisle of the bus, then he looked into his hand and counted the change the driver had given him. Immediately he saw that a mistake had been made so he went back and handed the dime to the driver, saying, "You gave me too much change." Then the driver said, "Yes, I intended to do that. I was testing you to see if you were a real Christian. I decided that if you kept that dime I would never go to church or listen to a preacher again. I believe now that there is some reality in religion."

Yes, honesty is the best policy. It is the only policy for a Christian.

IX. "Thou Shalt Not Bear False Witness"

Doesn't that mean just plain lying? God thinks that lying is wicked. He puts it right along with stealing, killing and committing adultery. Why did you tell that lie in your business? Why did you tell that lie when you answered the phone? Why did you tell that lie when you were talking to your neighbor?

Oh, the tongue is a little member of the body, but so is the fang of the rattlesnake. They both do great harm. Sometimes you hear a story about someone. You don't check up on it to see if it is true. You add a little to it, you pass it on. It hurts someone else. I have heard people say, "Did you hear about so-and-so? I am so sorry." No, they are not.

They are glad to hear it, for then they can go ahead and spill out the whole dirty mess and enjoy telling it.

Some years ago a serviceman and his wife started coming to our church. Before long they gave their hearts to Christ, were baptized and became faithful members. They came to church every time the door was opened. Then suddenly the man stopped coming and I wondered why. One night I went to see him and he gave me the old excuse of having to work too hard. Later his wife told me the real reason why he quit coming to church. A man who had formerly worked for the church took this serviceman down in the basement one day and gossiped about the pastor for an hour while his wife waited for him. That man said that he would never come back here to church again. Later on the man who had done the talking wrote a letter and apologized for what he had done, but the damage had been done. The serviceman never came back to church. Oh, what damage can be done by the tongue!

Dr. James McGinlay tells about being a guest in a home where the young son of the home was unsaved. The father seemed greatly concerned about his son's salvation. But at the dinner table Dr. McGinlay said that he heard this father criticize the church and the pastor and the leadership of the church. Then he said to himself, "That's the reason that the boy is unsaved." I have seen this thing scores of times. If you want to do the most damage to the spiritual life of your children, just keep on criticizing the preacher and the church in their presence. Every Christian ought to pray, "Oh, God, help me to control my tongue."

X. "Thou Shalt Not Covet"

To covet means to long for, to pant after, to set one's heart on that which belongs to another. Covetousness leads to all kinds of sin. It leads to stealing. A man covets something which belongs to another and soon he is so obsessed with this desire that he steals that thing. Covetousness leads to murder. A man covets another man's wife and kills to get her. Covetousness leads to adultery. A few years ago a prominent Hollywood actress went to Europe to make a picture. The director of the picture coveted her. This led to adultery, to an illegitimate child and divorce. Later on that union was broken up. It all began with covetousness.

The Bible tells us how to cure covetousness. It says, "Set your heart upon things above." It says, "Be content with the things that you have." So let us fill our hearts with Christ and throw covetousness out forever.

Yes, all of us have been weighed in the balances and found wanting. Why? Because we have not kept the laws of God perfectly. Is there any hope for us? Ah, yes, the One who died on the cross is our hope. Take Him into your side of the scales and all will be well. He is the only One who can settle our debt to the law. When you come to Him you may have ten thousand black marks against you. God looks on you as a lost sinner. But when you trust Him, all of your sins are washed away and all the black marks are erased. "The blood of Jesus Christ, His Son, cleanses us from all sin" and furnishes us transportation to heaven.

Do you remember the story of the Harlem railway bridge keeper? He received a message one day telling him that a special train would be coming down the track at a certain time. He was not to open the bridge for any purpose. It was to be kept closed so that the train could pass quickly and safely over. But a few minutes before the train was to arrive he heard the whistle of a tugboat and he was requested to open the bridge so the tugboat could pass down the river. He felt that he had plenty of time, so he opened up the bridge and the tugboat went through. Then he began to work the machinery which would bring the bridge back into place. But some part of the machinery failed and he could not get the bridge back into position for the train to pass over it. He worked furiously with the bridge to no avail. Then he heard the special train coming.

He tried to flag it down, but the engineer, thinking that he had a clear track ahead, came on speeding toward the bridge. The train plunged into the river and many lives were lost. The bridge keeper was under fifty years of age, but his hair turned gray in a short time. He lost his mind and had to be put in a padded cell. He would walk up and down his cell, crying out, "Oh, if I only had. If I only had." Then he would throw himself down upon his bed and cry out again, "Oh, if I only had."

Dear friend without Christ, if you go through life without a Saviour and go down to that awful place called hell, you will look back upon every opportunity that you had to become a Christian and throughout eternity you will be crying out in remorse, "Oh, if I only had. Oh, if I only had." With all my heart I plead with you to surrender to Jesus Christ today. He will be your best Friend for time and eternity, for this world and the world that is to be. He will see you through this life and take you home to heaven at the end of the way.

12

A Glimpse of His Glory

Matthew 17:1-12

The people who saw Jesus on earth never caught sight of His real glory. They saw Him heal the sick, cast out devils and raise the dead to life again. Yet as they looked upon Him they saw Him only as a man, a very wonderful man indeed, yet just a man. There is coming a day when all the world will see Him in all of His glory. This will be when He comes to earth again. Men will not see Him then as a servant, but as a great conquering King, robed in all the light and power and glory of heaven.

But one day three men did catch a glimpse of that glory. Jesus took Peter and James and John to the top of a high mountain and there He was transfigured. He was made the same as when He lived in glory with God the Father. His face shone like the sun and His raiment was as white as light. Moses and Elijah came down and talked with Him. They talked about Calvary and the death that He would die upon the cross. Peter was so entranced by this scene that he cried out, "Lord, let us stay up here and build three tabernacles, one for you, one for Moses and one for Elijah." Suddenly a bright cloud surrounded Him and a voice coming out of the clouds said, "This is my Beloved Son. Hear ye Him." The disciples fell upon their faces. They could not stand to look upon all of this glory. Then Jesus lifted them up and they saw no man "save Jesus only." Now there is the text, "They saw no man save Jesus only." There are two precious truths in this text. We see Jesus here, both as the solitary One and as the sufficient One.

I. The Solitude of the Saviour

1. *He was alone in His birth.* While the Virgin Mary
was praying a bright light shone around about her. She
opened her eyes and saw the angel Gabriel standing before
her. She shrank back in fear, but Gabriel reassured her,
saying, "You have found great favor with God. You are
going to bear a son and His Name shall be Jesus. He shall
be the greatest of the great. Indeed He shall be the Son
of God Himself." But Mary was puzzled so the angel said
unto her, "Do not worry about the matter. God's Holy
Spirit shall speak the child into being. Just leave it all to
Him." And Mary bowed her head and said, "Behold, I am
the hand-maiden of the Lord. Let it be unto me according
to thy will." Mary knew that shame and disgrace might
follow. But she was fully dedicated to God and she entered
into the plan without fear. The months pass by and she
marries Joseph. However, the Bible plainly tells us that
there were no marital relations between them. Then one
starry night the Lord Jesus Christ was born in a stable in
the little town of Bethlehem.

Jesus was the only child ever born of a virgin. Now
Mary was a good woman, but she was a sinner just as all
human beings are. Yet her Son was sinless. In Job 25:4 we
read, "How can he be clean (of sin) who is born of a
woman?" How then did it happen that Jesus was born
without sin? Here is the answer . . . . The Holy Spirit laid
hold of a part of Mary's body and purified it as a chemist
purifies metal. Thus He was born without sin.

When Jesus came down from heaven He brought with
Him His whole un-sinning nature. He was the sinless God.
He came to the world in a sinless body. Not so with us.
We are born in sin and we have a sinful nature. When the
devil tempted Jesus there was no response. There was nothing in Jesus that he could lay hold on. But when the devil
tempts us, even though we are saved, he has a little ter-
ritory in us that he can lay hold on. Our sinful nature is

still there. Jesus had a divine Father and a human mother. When He was born He completed the union between Deity and humanity. He brought God down to us and lifted us up to God. He was alone in His birth. There has never been another one like it in the history of the world.

2. *He was alone in His childhood.* His mother and his brothers did not understand the mystery which surrounded Him. At the age of twelve He rebuked His mother by saying, "Don't you know that I must be about my Father's business?" There must have been times when many children crowded around Him, yet He was truly alone in the crowd. You can feel alone in the midst of a million people if there is no common spirit there with whom to have fellowship.

Often when you try to live for Christ your loved ones do not understand. They ridicule you, they call you a sissy. They criticize your efforts to serve Christ. Often you will be lonely, yet you can always have the companionship of the greatest Friend in heaven and earth. You can always hear Him saying, "Fear thou not, for I am with thee. Be not dismayed for I am thy God."

3. *Jesus was alone in His ministry.* "He came to His own and His own received Him not." The doors of the world closed upon Him. He was the great unwanted One. He said that the foxes had holes and the birds of the air had nests, but that He had no place to lay His head. No one offered Him their hospitality. He spent the night on Olivet and as He looked down upon the twinkling lights of the city He sobbed out, "O Jerusalem, Jerusalem, how often would I have gathered thy children together, even as a hen gathereth her chickens under her wings, and ye would not!"

As He prayed in the Garden of Gethsemane He could cry out, "There is no sorrow like unto my sorrow." He tread the winepress alone. Even on the cross He was forsaken, for we hear Him crying, "My God, my God, why hast thou forsaken me?" Yes, He was alone all through His life.

4. *He was alone in the object of His death*. The two thieves who hung by Him could well say, "We are here because of our sins." But Jesus was the sinless One, dying for others. No one on this earth ever wholly died for others. Jesus was alone in this. The greatest souls of the world are those who have known solitude. Moses spent forty years in the land of Midia. Paul spent two years in Arabia before entering his public ministry. But Jesus stands alone as the great solitary Man. There has never been one like Him. There is no one on earth like Him now. There never will be one like Him.

II. The Sufficiency of the Saviour

When the disciples opened their eyes they saw Jesus only. Now they might have seen Moses only. There was a great deal of attraction about Moses. He was the great law giver of the Old Testament. But law is not enough to save us. Some people guide their lives by rules and duties and prohibitions. All they see in God's Word is a "thou shalt not." They try to guide other lives in the same way. They set themselves up as judges of righteousness. They know nothing of love and tolerance and sympathy. Don't get the idea that everyone is bad in the world except you. Don't try to apply the law to everyone else. Moses and the law are not enough.

They might have seen Elijah only. He represented the prophets. The true Bible scholar loves prophecy, but he sees something else in the Bible other than prophecy. We ought to preach prophecy in a sane way, to comfort and to give hope and assurance. But people get mighty tired if a preacher talks about Daniel and the Millennium and the man of sin every Sunday. We need to be well balanced in our religious thinking. We are not to major on Moses or Elijah, but on Jesus Christ. He is sufficient. In Him is all law and all prophecy. In Him is all that we need for time and eternity.

1. *Jesus is sufficient in salvation.* He is "able to save unto the uttermost all those who come unto Him by faith." We are not to take Jesus plus anything else, but Jesus only. He can save without the help of the church, a creed or a baptism. "He that believeth on the Son hath life, but he that believeth not on the Son hath not life, but the wrath of God abideth on him."

Some people want to feel that good works have something to do with salvation. But we work for God because we are saved and not in order to be saved. Why is it that many church members do nothing for the Lord? They never darken the door of the church, they never give, they never serve. It must be that they have never been saved. Surely if a man has been saved, he wants to do something for the Lord. But we must forever remember that we are not saved by our good works.

Men are not saved by a reformation, by turning over a new leaf. You are not saved by cutting off this sin or that bad habit. No, Jesus is the only saving One. An English preacher served during the war as a chaplain in France. One day when the men were absent he went into the dugout and over every bed he found an obscene picture or an impure quotation. His first impulse was to tear these things down, but then he said to himself, "These things do not belong to me and I have no right to tamper with them." He then went back to his own quarters and secured a beautiful picture of Jesus Christ. He went down to the dugout and pinned this picture in a prominent place, where the men could not help but see it. Later when the men came back they felt an invisible presence. Without a word to one another they tore down the dirty pictures. Nothing was left but the picture of Christ. That's the way it ought to be in the matter of salvation. We don't get a man saved by tear-ing down a few bad things in his life, but by presenting Christ who is sufficient in salvation.

When Paul went to Thessalonica he found idolatry on every side. He did not tell the people that they should be ashamed of themselves. He just told them about Christ. Then we read, "They turned to God from idols." A man in Canada had been a slave to drink for twenty-nine years. Someone persuaded him to go and hear J. Wilbur Chapman preach. When the invitation was given this man walked down the aisle and climbed up on the platform. He said, "Friends, I am climbing out of hell. You must help me." He was gloriously saved. Any man who comes to Jesus will find that He can save unto the uttermost.

2. *Jesus is sufficient in the time of temptation.* Before a man can really help another who is in trouble, he first must have had experience in the same trouble. Jesus has had experience in the matter of temptation. He knocked Satan out every time that he faced him. He is on our side when we, too, come face to face with temptation. Two things cannot occupy the same place at the same time. If we have Christ in our hearts, if we surrender completely to Him, the devil cannot get hold of us. A good old Christian man lived a life that was so fine that it made people marvel. A young man said to him one time, "What is the secret of your life? Are you ever bothered by temptation? Does the devil ever knock at the door of your heart?" "Oh, yes," answered the old man, "but when he knocks at the door of my heart I say to him, 'This space is occupied.'" It is true, if Jesus fills your heart the devil can't get in.

When Napoleon was engaged in the battle of Waterloo, he kept looking for Blucher to bring up reinforcements. These reinforcements never came and the battle was lost. We lose many battles, not because the forces are not there, but because we do not call upon them. Jesus is always ready to come to our aid. Why did David sin so greatly? It was because he looked upon sin and forgot about God.

How often that happens to us. But the charm of the name of Jesus drives away temptation.

> Take the name of Jesus with you
> As a shield from every snare,
> When temptations round you gather,
> Breathe that holy name in prayer.

3. *Jesus is sufficient in satisfying life.* He created the human heart and he knows how to satisfy it. The man who makes the motor knows how to repair it. The man who makes a lock fashions the key. Well, Jesus made us. He knows how to satisfy us. He knows how to bind up our broken hearts. He knows how to unlock every mystery and bring His children into the light. Augustine said, "We were made for Him and we are restless until we find peace in Him." It doesn't take Jesus and something else to satisfy us, but simply Jesus only.

A certain man went to see a millionaire. This rich man showed him his million dollar home, his cluster of automobiles, his large flower garden and his collection of birds. Then with a face filled with despair the rich man said, "Is there anything in the world that will give a man satisfaction?" His visitor happened to be a true Christian and he replied, "Yes, yield your life to Jesus Christ. He can fully satisfy." You can have everything in the world except Christ, but without Him you can never be permanently satisfied.

4. *Jesus is sufficient in sorrow and adversity.* Dr. John G. Paton and his young wife went to be missionaries among a group of cannibals. They looked forward to a happy life, but God willed otherwise. She died after a few months' of service in that faraway land. With his own hands Dr. Paton made the grave and buried his loved one. As he turned away from the grave, he heard the shouts of the cannibals. They were out to kill him, and he had to flee for his life. Later on he said, "If it had not been for Jesus, I would have gone mad."

Many of you have pressed the cup of agony to your own lips. You remember the hour when your loved one slipped away. The bottom fell out and life seemed to be empty. All of your plans and dreams were destroyed and the sun set on every hope. In those dark days much human sympathy was offered to you, but that did not ease the aching sorrow. Oh, but One stood by you to give you peace and songs in the night and grace and strength and courage for the hours ahead. It was Jesus. He is sufficient in the time of sorrow.

Yes, Jesus is sufficient for every need. He comes in the heart and never leaves. He is there to comfort, to bless, to guide, to forgive, to bring peace and hope. Is He yours today? Are you following Him? Is He all in all to you? Are you permitting Him to have His way in your life?

Dr. Len G. Broughton, on a certain Sunday, preached in the pulpit of an aristocratic church in the city of New York. There were only four people in the choir. Dr. Broughton said that he felt that they didn't have much spirituality and that they would not add much to the service. Then he saw a woman come down toward the front and take a seat over against the wall. She looked like a whipped child. The choir members whispered to each other when they saw her. Dr. Broughton preached his sermon and did an unusual thing for that church. He gave an invitation. This woman began to weep and soon she left her seat, ran down the aisle and fell on her knees at the altar. Dr. Broughton tried to talk to her and out of the corner of his eye he saw the four members of the choir leave the choir loft. He thought that they were disgusted with what had happened, but in a few seconds the side door opened and the four choir members came and knelt around this woman. They talked and prayed together and soon her tears were wiped away and she was happy in God's forgiveness. Later one of the members of the choir explained the situation to Dr. Broughton. He said, "This woman formerly sang in our choir. She had a beautiful voice which she used for the glory of God. But one day the devil tempted her and she went out from us. We have been praying for her ever since. This morning when we saw her come in we agreed that we would pray for her all the time that you were speaking. I am glad to say that God answered our prayers."

Dear friend, have you wandered away from God? Jesus is sufficient for your every need. He wants to love you and forgive you and bless you. Let me urge you to come to Him now.